The nursing profession is a t for those who believe in G(
grace. *Amazing Stories of Li*
excellent portrayal of how the nursing profession
and the spiritual disciple intermingle. You will be
uplifted in reading how Christ honestly plays a
role in so many lives each day, in so many different ways—you just have to open your eyes and
your heart to accept.

—Beverly Essick, RNC MSN
Former Director of Health Education/
Nursing Instructor at
Surry Community College

Amazing Stories of Life After Death is captivating
and compelling proof that God is indeed still
at work in the lives of people on Planet Earth.
Reading these real-life experiences from a medical professional, a person of science and also of
faith, strengthened my personal faith. I have read
this book several times, and each time I was so
captivated by these personal experiences I was
not able to put the book down until I reached the
final page. This book will touch your heart and
strengthen your faith.

—Mark Donovan, PhD
Founder and Senior Pastor of Donovan
International Christian Ministries, Inc.

Amazing Stories of Life After Death, written by Liz
Gwyn, illustrates that our God is still here with
us in our time of need. These true-life experiences
are refreshing and uplifting to read. Having such
stories to read strengthens our beliefs in the true

meaning of faith. This book will certainly touch your heart and reinforce your faith.

—SHARYN N. CONRAD, DNP, APRN, FNP-BC
ASSISTANT PROFESSOR OF NURSING
WINSTON-SALEM STATE UNIVERSITY

Amazing Stories of Life After Death is a gift that you will never forget once you read. Having experienced some of these incidents as an emergency nurse, I was compelled to read this book in one sitting until the last page. *Amazing Stories of Life After Death* will allow you to see through the eyes of a faith-believing nurse as she experiences her patients' walk through illness, healing, death, and beyond. It will indeed bless you and strengthen your personal belief as we are only here for a short time before our real lives begin with our heavenly Father.

—DR. SUSAN THORNTON
ASSISTANT PROFESSOR OF NURSING
WINSTON-SALEM STATE UNIVERSITY

It is a pleasure to recommend this book of inspiration, hope, and factual evidence that everyday miracles still happen to ordinary people. Faith and willingness to listen for God's voice are as obvious in the true stories as in the life of the author. Through the lens of a Christian nurse educator, Liz Gwyn offers the reader a glimpse into extraordinary events.

—CATHY HINSON FRANKLIN-GRIFFIN,
PHD, MSN, RN, CHPN
ASSISTANT PROFESSOR OF NURSING & INTERIM
DIRECTOR OF RN-BSN OPTION
WINSTON-SALEM STATE UNIVERSITY

Amazing Stories *of*
LIFE
after
Death

Amazing Stories of
LIFE
after
Death

LIZ GWYN, MSN, RN

CHARISMA
HOUSE

Most CHARISMA HOUSE BOOK GROUP products are available at special quantity discounts for bulk purchase for sales promotions, premiums, fund-raising, and educational needs. For details, write Charisma House Book Group, 600 Rinehart Road, Lake Mary, Florida 32746, or telephone (407) 333-0600.

AMAZING STORIES OF LIFE AFTER DEATH
    by Liz Gwyn, MSN, RN
Published by Charisma House
Charisma Media/Charisma House Book Group
600 Rinehart Road
Lake Mary, Florida 32746
www.charismahouse.com

Unless otherwise noted, all Scripture quotations are from the Amplified Bible. Old Testament copyright © 1965, 1987 by the Zondervan Corporation. The Amplified New Testament copyright © 1954, 1958, 1987 by the Lockman Foundation. Used by permission.

Scripture quotations marked KJV are from the King James Version of the Bible.

Scripture quotations marked NIV are from the Holy Bible, New International Version. Copyright © 1973, 1978, 1984, International Bible Society. Used by permission.

Names and details of the stories in this book have been changed to protect the privacy of the individuals.

Cover design by Bill Johnson

Visit the author's website at http://amazingstories2012.com/.

Library of Congress Cataloging-in-Publication Data
Gwyn, Liz.
Amazing stories of life after death / Liz Gwyn. -- 1st ed.
p. cm.
Includes bibliographical references (p.).
ISBN 978-1-61638-612-2 (trade paper) -- ISBN 978-1-61638-720-4 (e-book)
1. Visions. 2. Supernatural. 3. Miracles. 4. Near-death experiences-
-Religious aspects--Christianity. I. Title.

BV5091.V6G99 2012
236'.1--dc23

2012011706

While the author has made every effort to provide accurate telephone numbers and Internet addresses at the time of publication, neither the publisher nor the author assumes any responsibility for errors or for changes that occur after publication.

First edition

12 13 14 15 16 — 9 8 7 6 5 4 3 2 1
Printed in the United States of America

To the Father, Son, and Holy Spirit—without whom there would be no story to tell.

To Timmy, Tabitha, Jessi, and Eddie. For all the times you listened to me tell the same stories over and over. You caught the vision and suffered through it with me. You are the most important people in my life.

To Roy, Dorothy, Barbara, Claude, Bonnie, and my family and friends. Just for being you.

In loving memory of my parents, Jesse Kyle Smith and Ruby Mae Hunter, my sweet cousin Danny Frank Willis, and my treasured friend Trena Barishnicov. You are forever in my heart.

CONTENTS

ACKNOWLEDGMENTS

I WOULD LIKE TO thank Charisma House for the opportunity to publish this book and to share the amazing stories of a nurse.

I would like to thank Leslie Stobbe for your expertise and willingness to work with "newbies." You listened.

I would like to thank Debbie Marrie and Jevon Bolden for vision and your passion for this project. Larry J. Leech II for your talents and compassionate heart. Keep the words of the Holy Spirit close to your heart, "He's my servant."

I would like to thank all my proofreaders and endorsers, especially Mark Donovan—you were patient and always willing to reread my manuscript no matter how many times I asked. Pastor Wayde and Rosalyn Goodall, and Joan Able for introducing me to television.

Thanks to Matt Marion, Todd Naylor, Jessi Gwyn, Jonathan Creed, the Lawson family, Cory, Audrey Leech, Dean Gammons, Sheri Jacobson, Sandra Lichvar, Tabatha Mauldin, Sharyn Conrad, and Christi Snow for sharing your stories. Cody Smith for always getting excited and texting faithfully to stay updated and encouraging me—I still feel sure we are family, from one Smith to another—LOL.

Thank you, New Century Church family, for praying and believing. Mamie Smith for crying when you heard I had a book contract—that's love. Clarence Smith—my favorite uncle. Karen Crotts, my heart is with you.

I give one last very special thanks to my friends Dr. Cathy Franklin-Griffin, Lori Hines, Bettie Little, Sandra

Wilder, Dorothy Stafford, Christina Hale, Dr. Susan Thornton, Dr. Lenora Campbell, Dr. Peggy Valentine, and Carol Boles. Cathy, we went through quite a time the year and a half I was working on this book. You were a godsend. I just hope I helped you a small portion—because your friendship helped me tremendously. Lori, what can I say, girl? If God had not connected us in such a special way, I wouldn't have had any food while writing this book. You will never know what you mean to me. God bless you forever. Bettie, Sandra, Susan, Beth, Christina, Dr. Campbell, and Dr. Valentine, thank you for getting *so* excited and yelling praises with each step of the publishing process—you made this experience double fun for me! Carol, you remembered me and made significant connections at the right time—for that I will always be grateful. Through you God handed me a very large gift. I will never forget your kindness and abundant generosity.

Dr. Davis stared at the floor as he spoke, 'Dean, some things in life we just don't understand....You are free to get up when you feel like it, and we'll have you out of here soon.' Just a few short hours earlier Dean's destiny was a wheelchair. Now he could go home?"

The story of Dean and many others in *Amazing Stories of Life After Death* has a familiar ring to it.

> A man crippled from birth was being carried to the temple gate called Beautiful, where he was put every day to beg from those going into the temple courts. When he saw Peter and John about to enter, he asked them for money. Peter looked straight at him, as did John. Then Peter said, "Look at us!"...Then Peter said, "Silver or gold I do not have, but what I have I give you. In the name of Jesus Christ of Nazareth, walk."... He jumped to his feet... went with them into the temple courts, walking, and jumping, and praising God.
>
> —Acts 3:2–8, niv

Miracles, healing, and gifts of the Holy Spirit are a great part of the work of God in these last days. People who depend on God to answer prayer and who want to listen to the voice of the Holy Spirit and use the gifts God has given them are beginning to become more and more common. *Amazing Stories of Life After Death* is an amazing testimony of a nurse who has permitted the Lord to use her in gifts of healing, discernment, words of wisdom, and courage to introduce others in her workplace and under her care to Jesus Christ.

As you read *Amazing Stories of Life After Death*, your faith will hopefully grow as you become encouraged to trust God for miracles and learn to listen to His quiet voice within you. God gives His gifts freely and can use you because you are also important in the body of Christ (1 Cor. 12:7).

As believers in Christ there are many gifts of the Holy Spirit that are available to us. Your life is not an accident. People whom God brings into your life are no mistake. God has created you "for such a time as this." Whether you are a nurse, educator, attorney, clergy person, or assistant in a grocery store, the Lord wants to use you in miraculous ways as you trust Him.

Reading this book will give you firsthand—present day—examples of how your faith and dependence on the Holy Spirit will bring you into people's lives so that you can give them hope, wisdom, and, for many, a unique word from God.

—Dr. Wayde Goodall
Dean, College of Ministry Northwest University
President, WorldWide Family. Inc.

A Reluctant Vessel

Nursing is one of the most dynamic professions in the world. According to the Bureau of Labor Statistics' Employment Projections 2010–2020 released in February 2012, the registered nursing workforce is the top occupation in terms of job growth through 2020. It is expected that the number of employed nurses will grow from 2.74 million in 2010 to 3.45 million in 2020, an increase of 712,000 or 26 percent. The projections further explain the need for 495,500 replacements in the nursing workforce, bringing the total number of job openings for nurses due to growth and replacements to 1.2 million by 2020.[1] Despite an economic recession, people continue to need health care and will need it in the coming years as a huge influx of baby boomers hit retirement age.

In this profession men and women alike can affect so many lives. A nurse is able to help people in the best of times—the birth of a child—and in the worst of times—impending death. We nurses have the unique ability to help someone whose life is hanging by a thread.

Nurses encourage and promote health for the healthy, sick, and all in between. In one day a nurse can touch as few as one life to as many as one hundred lives. This includes not only the patient but also family and friends.

So why do we care for patients and comfort and encourage their family and friends? I frequently ask students why they want to be a nurse and practicing nurses why they chose this profession. It's not easy to get into nursing school. The criteria for acceptance challenge applicants and the competition for admission is high. When I teach, I ask this question during the first day of class, and I receive a variety of answers. First-year students are a bundle of energy and nerves after being accepted into school. Some say they want a better life financially for their families. Others admit they were inspired by the tenderness of a nurse who cared for a family member in the final days before passing away. Still others say they wanted to be a nurse since they were children. One exasperated new baccalaureate graduate bluntly said, "Money!" After four to five years of being in nursing school, I'm sure she needed money.

"THIS JOB ISN'T FOR ME. I'M LEAVING."

Many years ago on my first day of nursing school, Beverly Essicks, who quickly became my favorite instructor, energetically said, "Welcome to nursing school. You are the elite…"

That's all I can remember of her welcome speech. I got stuck on the words "You are the elite." I had no idea I could be elite at anything! Being raised in a dysfunctional family, I never learned how precious I was to God. I didn't learn that until years later when I fully gave my life over to Him.

Those four words carried me through the next two agonizing years of reading, studying, mass paperwork, tests, clinical, and being broke and separated from family and friends.

Though it is common for people to have legitimate reasons for wanting to be a nurse, I must admit I did not. A couple of years after high school I worked at the sock factory in Mount Airy. My job was to put socks onto a really hot board (like putting them on feet) to press them for packaging. It was repetitive, boring, and I burned myself a lot. I realized this was not a career for me.

Someone mentioned I could probably get financial help to attend college, so I didn't waste any time in starting my search. I soon discovered they were right. A short time later I heard someone else say nursing was a career that paid well. Honestly, I had no idea what nurses did. I had never been sick or spent any time in a hospital with a sick family member. Having come from a less-than-fortunate family, the pursuit of a financially lucrative career appealed to me.

I couldn't wait to get through school and into the workforce so I could have money—money to buy things, to eat where I wanted, to spoil my husband and my children, to live in a nice home and drive a really nice car.

But first I had to get through English, reading, anatomy and physiology, and a certified nursing assistance course. I did well in everything but anatomy and physiology. I made a C—a far cry from my normal As and Bs I was accustomed to making in high school. Anatomy and physiology was by far the hardest course I had ever taken, and I had an epiphany. During the twelve-week course I realized I didn't like learning about chemistry and the physiology of the human body. I finished the course but knew in my heart that nursing wasn't for me. No amount of money could entice me to change my mind.

Much to my surprise and against what I felt were my best interests, I did find a job in the nursing field—as a certified nurse assistant in a nursing home. I lasted less than three whole months. I even had the gall to confront the director of nursing and tell her, "This job isn't for me. I'm leaving." And I did—in the middle of my shift. Well, anyone who is a nurse and is reading this knows you just don't do that. A licensed nurse will lose her license to practice if she abandons her shift—which means she abandoned her patients. Thankfully, I was a nurse assistant, not a registered nurse. Still, leaving in the middle of the shift with patients who needed me was a horrible thing to do. I know better now, but back then, you might say, I was a little young and careless. I've grown up a little—well, a lot—since that time.

It took another two years before I came full circle back to nursing school. I really didn't want to be a nurse or a doctor. Neither of those careers appealed to me. But I knew I needed to figure out something because factory work wasn't for me. I was unsure of a career choice, so I didn't have a clue as to what I should study in college.

I was in my early twenties, I was working in a factory—again—and I was sure there had to be more to life than putting screws into toasters. I couldn't picture myself doing that for the rest of my life. I knew I should go to college, but I had no idea what field to pursue as a career.

BUT GOD...

One evening my husband picked me up from work. As we were approaching a red light, I had a vision. For a moment the scene opened up before me. I saw six people, including me, standing around a hospital bed. We all wore long white lab coats and were looking down at the person in the bed and discussing something important.

Confused, I thought to myself, "God, are You trying to tell me You want me to be a doctor?" I thought about it and decided that wasn't possible. I didn't want to be a doctor, and I couldn't imagine affording medical school without God's supernatural provision.

I carefully considered the vision and decided I would go to nursing school instead. I enrolled in a local college and applied for entrance into the nursing program. Six months later I received an acceptance letter. The remarkable thing was that only 65 students were accepted among 365 applicants. I planned to start with nursing school and pursue medical school sometime later, when I might be able to afford it.

Fifteen years later I found myself walking across the street at a local hospital in a long white lab coat. I was on my way to teach new nursing students the clinical portion of patient care. I stepped onto the pavement as I had done regularly for the previous two years when the Holy Spirit flashed the vision of the lab coats and bed before my eyes and said, "You are here."

This excited me because I had been questioning whether I was following God's will for my life. Thoughts of my need to return to school to obtain a post-master nurse practitioner certificate nagged at me because I still couldn't afford to go to medical school.

Our Father's insights can amaze us. I felt as though a tremendous weight had been lifted from me. Now I could focus on what God wanted me to do next. I realized I was on track, but I knew I shouldn't stop there. He always has more.

Of course we shouldn't interpret all dreams and visions as direct messages from God, but we must understand that He does speak to us in this way. We shouldn't discount anything the Holy Spirit says to us. We have such limited time on earth, and every breath counts. Our desire must be to follow as God leads us.

AN ACT OF OBEDIENCE

The *second* time I went to college for nursing school was not because I wanted to be a nurse. It was an act of obedience for what I believed to be an instruction from God. And believe me, it was an act of obedience.

I was terrified of blood, feces, urine, sputum—anything and everything that excretes from the body. Worst than that, I was—still am—afraid of death.

Going back for the second time didn't make the course load easier. It was still hard. This time, however, I made As in the anatomy and physiology classes. My goal was to make As and Bs as I worked toward my associate degree. I remember only one C. That was in the final Adult Health course of the program—famous for being the "make-it-or-fail-you" course.

The pressure of being a nursing student is nothing compared to being a nurse. Being a nurse is the hardest thing I have ever done. After I received my degree, I went to work every day terrified that I would make a mistake or that someone would die on me. It's inevitable that people will make mistakes, and I certainly was no exception. It's inevitable that people will die, and I took care of patients who did.

For eleven years I dealt with those fears. I often wondered why God called me into the medical field when I never did fit the mold. I've met only one other nurse like me since I started in this profession nearly two decades ago. Everyone else I have spoken to admits they love the hype of emergency, critical care, too much to do, and so on. These people are true nurses in every sense of the word. It's what they live for. Not me. I was restless. I needed something else, so I decided to become a traveling nurse. At least changing locations every few weeks helped me stay challenged and in the field longer. Little did I know that all of my nursing experiences and the heavy stress would one day lead to this book.

I often have thought back to a turning point in my career and my life. One day while working at a travel assignment as a post-anesthesia care unit nurse in a Tennessee hospital, I said, "Lord, I am so tired of this stress. I've done this for years. How much longer?"

I heard in my spirit lyrics from the song "Ooh Child" by the Five Stairsteps.

Yes, the Holy Spirit sang that old secular song to me. The sweet words of the song lifted my spirits, and I was able to hang on because I knew better days were coming. And they couldn't arrive fast enough. At that point my goal was to retire from nursing nearly thirty years early. And although I didn't have the nice nest of years of service to really retire, I couldn't take the stress any longer. At this point flipping burgers at a fast-food joint seemed like a wonderful option. Or maybe serving up lattes at a local coffeehouse. I was so ready for things to get easier!

Like most things with God, His timing was a little different from mine. While I wanted the change to begin sooner rather than later, circumstances did start soon after to set me on a different path. A few weeks after hearing the Holy Spirit sing "Ooh Child," I received an e-mail from my sister Dorothy about an opportunity that piqued my interest. She had been doing research on the Internet for a medical secretary instructor job after finishing a two-year degree for medical office administration. At one point during her search, she ended up on the site of a community college in North Carolina. There she found a listing for a nursing instructor. Knowing I was looking to get out of the nursing profession, she sent me a link to the job description. I scoffed at the idea of teaching. Most colleges want nurses with a master's degree and teaching experience. I didn't have either. This position, however, required a bachelor's degree with preference of a master's degree. After praying for a few days and talking it over with my husband, Tim, I applied. I didn't get my hopes up. I knew it was a long shot, at best, but I had to at least try.

Three weeks later, after we moved from Tennessee to North Carolina for my husband, Tim, to start a new church, I got a call from the community college requesting an interview. I couldn't believe it. I had given up on the teaching opportunity and taken a home care job when we moved. I really wanted to teach, but I was torn over the possibility of leaving my new job if I received an offer from the college. If I left, the company would have lost money for training me. I decided I couldn't pass on the teaching opportunity, so I went for the interview and was offered the job one week later. Although I had a fear of public speaking, I accepted the position, and for the next two and a half years I joyfully sang the song the Holy Spirit sang over me months earlier.

I couldn't believe it. I finally had found a purpose for all the hard times and years as a practicing nurse. I was to teach others what I had learned during fifteen years of being in the field. But that wasn't the end of my pressure and stretching. State requirements changed. Nursing instructors had three years to get a master's degree in nursing or a special certificate to continue teaching. I went back to get my master's degree, and as soon as I graduated, my world in nursing education started falling apart.

More pressure came. My mother died. And my boss at the community college took a position at another college. My husband lost his salary. He didn't lose his position as a pastor, but the church plant lost two major supporters and the recession hit, dramatically decreasing the amount of two tithes coming in. His salary went from $1,800 a month to zero. Zip. Nada. His loss of income strapped us financially and emotionally.

So I tried to get a nursing instructor position at the closest university. Working conditions at the community college were difficult under the new boss, and I was completely burnt out. Staying at the community college wouldn't bring in enough money. We needed more. So I looked for three things in a new job: opportunity, promotion in the field of education, and higher salary. Universities pay better than community colleges, so moving up would allow me to make up for the loss of Tim's salary. I failed. The country was in the middle of a recession. And we couldn't sell our house.

Stress from my personal life and from the job was taking a toll on me. Between my boss being difficult and me being burned out, things had changed too much for me at the community college. I no longer felt like I was benefiting the school or the students. I knew the Lord was moving me from the community college, but I was terrified to let go of my salary. In my desperate state I cried out to God one evening, "Show me what to do, God, and I will do it." While reading the Bible that evening, I learned from John 12:49–50 that Jesus Himself never did anything without instructions from the Father. There was no more room for guessing. I needed an answer, and I needed it quick.

THE BOOK

I got my answer that very night. The Lord told me to write a book. At first I reasoned with Him, saying I didn't know anything about writing a book. He insisted. I obeyed. In the middle of all that pressure, this book was birthed. Night after night He reminded me of the super-ordinary ordeals I experienced during my fifteen years of staff nursing. I would get up the next day and write out the stories. I couldn't believe God was pouring the most stressful times of my nursing career into a book.

I held on to the community college position for three more months. Miserable and knowing what had to be done, I—to use a worn out cliché—let go and let God. Finally the Holy Spirit told me to stop running the out-of-control race in my life and I would *see* God. Meaning I would see Him do great things without my salary.

The pressure became so great that I knew it was time to make a change despite my fears. So I resigned without having a full-time job lined up. Only an insane person would do something like that in the middle of a recession—or someone who had finally learned to have complete faith and trust while being obedient. I like to think I'm the latter.

We may not be able to understand why we are going through hard times or why we have to make changes that really make no sense. But when we have the heart to follow the leading of the Holy Spirit, He will lead us into greater things. We will go through a lot of pressure to get there though.

EMBRACE YOUR SEASON

I shared all this to say you may feel that your job as a waitress, flight attendant, certified nurse assistant, janitor, president of a corporation, physician, pastor, pastor's wife, mother, or wherever you are is meaningless. But it may be the means to another season in your life. Life has seasons.

Your first season of adult life may be college or marriage and a family. Your second season may be your career and/or providing for your family. Your third season may be more growth—going back to school; recovering from a broken relationship; or death of parents, friends, or family members. Your fourth season may be doing something you have never done before, using all of the previous seasons of growth and experience to get there.

Each season has a reason and a specific purpose. Prayerfully go through the seasons. Nothing comes easy that is worth having. Everything takes time and hard work. Be faithful; follow God. You will start to see why you are on the course you are on in due time. The Bible says do not faint and grow weary with well doing (Gal. 6:9). In due time you will bear fruits, and in more time you will enjoy those fruits. No pressure produces no results. Little pressure produces little results. Moderate pressure produces moderate results. Great pressure produces great results.

We can see evidence of this in the media coverage of Sara Palin, ex-governor of Alaska and John McCain's running mate in the failed GOP bid for the White House in 2008. She progressed from a woman virtually unknown to anyone except Alaskans to a public figure known throughout the world.

She endured *lots* of pressure as she progressed through this pivotal season of her life. During that time we have had the privilege of seeing many sides of her personality: competitive, serious, happy, playful, and angry. We've heard the fire in her voice during her speeches. She has been put under intense pressure, but all that great pressure has produced great results. With great confidence and assurance, she handles all criticism of her and her family with great grace.

Talk about growth—in just a few short years. In many ways we've seen her grow up right before our eyes—in the public eye, which is not an easy thing to do.

Some people, such as Palin, can handle the pressure with grace. Some can't. Just think of someone from the long list of Hollywood superstars who have self-destructed the last couple of years. Somewhere and somehow the pressure became too great for them. With God great pressure will produce great results. Patience and endurance are the key.

Imagine what kind of pressure we'd endure if we were the president of a country. Have you noticed how nearly every US president turns gray during his time in office? President Clinton comes to mind. When he first took office in 1993, he had a full head of dark hair. When he left eight years later, he was completely gray.

Billy Graham, often called the pastor to presidents, is a fine example of a person's ability to handle pressure with grace. Graham rose to celebrity status as his sermons were broadcast on radio and television, beginning in the late 1940s. A Gallup poll ranks him number seven on the list of the most admired people of the twentieth century.

It is believed Graham has preached the gospel in person to more people than any other person in history. According to his staff, as of 1993 more than 2.5 million people have "stepped forward at his crusades to accept Christ as their personal Savior."[2] Graham's lifetime audience, including radio and television broadcasts, topped 2 billion, according to a special section about Graham in the *Cincinnati Post*.[3]

During the height of his popularity, which included preaching at numerous outdoor stadiums during the 1970s, Graham, like Palin, was under intense scrutiny. While Graham went to great lengths to live a godly life, we have seen what happens when others have made mistakes. We must admit mistakes lead to intense pressure, and how we handle them will make or break us—whether we are in the public eye or not.

GOD SEES THE GOLD IN US

No one who grows will grow without pressure. We may not always like the process, but the process molds us and fits us into His purpose. We may not like the job we have. We may not like where we live. We may not like our financial situation. But when we are following God and we know we have heard from Him, He will take our sacrificial offerings of obedience and turn them into gold. All in time.

Sadly we may talk ourselves out of the gold to come.

We may rationalize and convince ourselves that God isn't really telling us to do something that we don't see ourselves doing, just as I didn't want to be a nurse. The entire time in the profession I never felt being a nurse fit who I was. If I had listened to my own understanding and had not gone through the pressure, I would not have met all the people I have. I would not have touched their lives; neither would they have touched mine.

If Jesus had chosen to "let this cup pass from Me," we would not have a Savior. He made a deliberate decision to be condemned, tortured, and to die so we could have a choice of spiritual life or death. So we could be free to worship God in spirit and in truth. So we could be alive spiritually and have access to all His wisdom and benefits. So we could be assured that we will live eternally. What if He had said, "Father, I don't think You would want Me to go to the cross for these people. They don't believe anything We say. They constantly bicker and complain. It's not for Me. I think I'll go." Then we would absolutely have no hope. Death would be a terror for us. Thank God He saw the gold—us—and endured the pressure.

Careers take a lot of work, and many times a person will give up on dreams because the work and commitment are much more than expected. These people abandon the pursuit of the dream when they have to give up too much in the process of preparation. I love what Thomas A. Edison said: "Opportunity is missed by most people because it is dressed in overalls and looks like work."[4]

You may feel the calling to be an astronaut or a lawyer. You may feel the calling to be a medical missionary or government official. You may feel your family and children are your calling. Whatever it is—your calling—stay true to what God puts in your heart. Nothing is impossible.

Whatever you are destined to do, God has equipped you to do. Pull up your sleeves, put on your best tennis shoes, and take off running. Press and press until you produce results.

Don't fear the pressure. Try to embrace it. Pressure does produce results. We may feel like the pressure is too great for us. We may feel like we are in the wrong place. We may feel like quitting. I felt like quitting every day of my clinical nursing days. Being a nurse is not glamorous; it's hard work.

I've had to face many things I was afraid of, but I see that God used these opportunities to work supernaturally in people's lives. I have had to be there with my patients when they transitioned from this life to the next. I have been their companion during the loneliest and most painful hours of their lives just to deliver a saving word to their soul. The hardest thing for me is to see people in pain and have fear in their eyes when they are facing the end of their lives. But God has used me to bring them hope, peace, and salvation through dreams, visions, and as a witness to the ministering aid of His angels. Amazingly there are still days I feel like I'm not making a difference in anyone's life. But I can also look back at some of the patients—Lacy Brown, Matt, Todd, Cassi, and others— under my care, and I have nice little reminders that I have made a difference in a number of lives.

In this book I will be sharing these stories and more. There will also be stories from my nursing friends and coworkers. Through all this I pray that you will be strengthened in your faith to know that whatever season you are in right now, God has a glorious plan for you. You are there for a purpose.

CHAPTER 1

Mr. Smith

But when He, the Spirit of Truth (the Truth-giving
Spirit) comes, He will guide you into all the Truth
(the whole, full Truth). For He will not speak His own
message [on His own authority]; but He will tell
whatever He hears [from the Father; He will give the
message that has been given to Him], *and He will
announce and declare to you the things that are to
come [that will happen in the future].*
—JOHN 16:13, EMPHASIS ADDED

IT IS IMPORTANT to be able to hear from God, even though as a nurse I am not able to actively share my faith. Some of what I have heard or seen in dreams or visions from God have prepared me to serve a patient in a way that changes their eternal destiny. Other times God has directed me on how to interact with a patient on a spiritual level so their lives on this earth are changed for the better. He has directed me so specifically to where He has even told me what to say and when to say it. It took a few "failed attempts" to help me develop my spiritual ears and eyes regarding this. Not all ended as well as I hoped, but I believe all of them worked out for the good of my patient, their families, and me.

In the mid-1990s I had a dream that helped me prepare for the passing of a patient I had never met. During the first of three days off my night started like every other. I ate dinner, cleaned up, put the kids to bed, and collapsed into bed, exhausted. During the night I had a dream that troubled me deeply.

In this night vision I walked into a male patient's hospital room to perform my morning assessment. The elderly gentleman lay on the bed, restless and short of breath. I noted the blue tinge of his lips. As I went about my routine of checking his vitals and IV bag, I added notes to his chart. Every few minutes he told me, "If I could just get up and walk in the hall, I would feel better."

At first I succeeded in convincing him he should rest. But a few minutes later his persistent pleas returned. He wanted to get out of bed. I finally relented and assisted him on a walk down the hall. After a short distance we were suddenly transported back to his room, where he went into cardiac arrest. Several medical staff members surrounded the bed and attempted to resuscitate him. While they worked, an invisible force lifted me onto the ledge at the foot of the bed that nurses and doctors use to write notes on charts. I sat there watching the team work on him, the whole time wanting to scream, "Just leave him alone; he's dead!"

But I couldn't scream. The words wouldn't leave my throat. I sat dumbfounded as my coworkers worked frantically on the man in their efforts to revive him.

While I struggled to scream, I sensed a presence enter the room. Immediately I lifted my hands into the air, like many people do when they worship. I'd never raised my hands in the air like this, but I couldn't control myself. Raising my hands high above my head and lifting my chin toward heaven suddenly felt as natural as breathing.

I quickly realized the presence of only one person could cause this reaction in me—Jesus. His presence was mighty and demanded my full attention. I drank in the beauty of His golden face and softness of His wooly, snow-white hair. I was in complete awe. Joy and peace filled the room. I clung to the feeling, never wanting to leave His presence.

With His eyes fixed on me, an opening appeared and hovered over the man on the bed. A long, thin vapor rose from the man's chest and disappeared through what I now realized was a spiritual window.

I awoke, troubled by this intense dream. I needed to share it with someone. So I rousted my husband, Tim, from his own sweet dreams. Groggily he listened to my frightful experience of watching a man die and the elation of being in the presence of the Lord. Neither of us understood the meaning. We prayed, asking the Lord to give me the knowledge I needed. Eventually I drifted back to sleep.

Two days later I returned to work. As usual I took my morning report and set out to care for my patients. When I entered my first patient's room I was shocked to see everything in living color like in my dream: the same man lying on the bed, restless, short of breath and with blue lips. I thought, "Oh, God, is this really happening?"

As I looked at Mr. Smith, I tried to sort through the jumbled thoughts bouncing around my brain like a bumblebee. I had to remain calm so I could do my job well. But I was terrified. I have a problem with death, which may seem odd for someone in the medical field. The thing is, I don't like to be in the room when a person passes. I try to avoid being in the room at all costs. Only a few times did I get stuck in the room, which made for some of the worst days of my nursing career.

I remembered the nurse on duty before me said Mr. Smith had a "do not resuscitate" (DNR) order. This particular DNR instructed us to avoid any lifesaving measures in the case of respiratory or cardiac arrest. A DNR can be specific in not allowing nurses and doctors to perform chest compressions; use a ventilator, life-saving medications, feeding tube, tracheotomy, or intravenous fluids; or a combination of any or all of these procedures. As I thought about all this, my stomach tightened.

I went about gathering the normal information we record during our rounds at the beginning of a shift along with making sure oxygen is flowing properly, IV lines are connected and working properly, and the patient is comfortable.

Trembling, I approached his bed and asked, "How are you doing, Mr. Smith?"

He replied through wheezy gasps, "I'm having a little trouble breathing. I think if I could just get up and walk down the hall, I'd feel better."

At his age and because of his condition, getting out of

the bed was the last thing he should do. Still trembling, I tried to keep my voice calm. I didn't want him to hear or see my anxiety as I encouraged him to stay in bed. I knew if he tried to walk, he would pass out.

In an attempt to assess his spiritual needs, I asked if he went to church anywhere. He responded, his voice suddenly strong, "I used to go to church a long time ago."

As I continued my assessment, his heart rate slowed to a dangerous level, one too low to sustain life. The normal range is between sixty and one hundred beats per minute. His had dropped to about thirty. I was in danger of watching him die. The dream I had three nights before was coming true—right before my eyes.

Although I knew we had no legal right to resuscitate him, I called for help—more for me than for the patient. I left the room to talk with the nurse manager while the other person who came to my rescue stayed with Mr. Smith. I explained to the manager that I couldn't continue to care for this patient because I was emotionally distraught. I told her about the dream. She replaced the nurse I called with another. This nurse took over the care of Mr. Smith during the final minutes of his life.

For the next thirty minutes I locked myself in the bathroom in an attempt to regain my composure. I spent half of the time sitting on the floor crying. Deep, heavy sobs racked my body. I'm a nurse, so I know how to handle almost anything. I don't often come unglued. But seeing my dream suddenly come to life shook me to the core.

When I pulled myself together, I made my way to the nurses' station and stood with my eyes focused on the central heart monitor. The monitor technologist and I watched my patient flatline. The steady, high-pitched squeal sent people flying into action.

I wondered how I would get through the rest of the day. I felt a little guilty about needing time to pull myself together, but I appreciated my manager's understanding in giving me the chance to regain my composure. It took some effort, but I managed to finish what was probably the most difficult shift of my career. And that includes the day I watched a seventy-year-old woman die from a massive gastrointestinal bleed. Blood poured out from every orifice, spilling onto the bed and floor. The entire team worked furiously to save her, with no success.

After Mr. Smith died, I kept to myself the rest of the day. I struggled at times with the knowledge that my dream had become a reality. Not until hours later when I got home did I begin to recover from the trauma. The tightness in my chest took days to dissipate.

I didn't realize at the time that God had used this dream to begin showing me things that would happen in the days ahead. I didn't understand at first that He could do this through dreams or visions. Although many people have trouble comprehending or believing the phenomenon of watching a night vision come true, I knew God had shown me this man's future in a dream.

God did this same thing when He sent a message to the prophet Isaiah to warn Hezekiah of his impending death. We read about the story in 2 Kings 20:1–5:

> In those days Hezekiah became deadly ill. The prophet Isaiah son of Amoz came and said to him, Thus says the Lord: Set your house in order, for you shall die; you shall not recover. Then Hezekiah turned his face to the wall and prayed to the Lord, saying, I beseech You, O Lord, [earnestly] remember now how I have walked before

You in faithfulness and truth and with a whole heart [entirely devoted to You] and have done what is good in Your sight. And Hezekiah wept bitterly. Before Isaiah had gone out of the middle court, the word of the Lord came to him: Turn back and tell Hezekiah, the leader of My people, Thus says the Lord, the God of David your [forefather]: I have heard your prayer, I have seen your tears; behold, I will heal you. On the third day you shall go up to the house of the Lord.

In this passage we see Hezekiah being warned by the prophet that his time on the earth was coming to an end. Isaiah told him that God said to set his house in order. Hezekiah took this warning seriously and quickly cried out to God, moving God's heart to extend his life fifteen more years.

This story proves why we cannot afford to ignore messages we receive in our spirit. Amazing things happen when we realize who our Father is, who Jesus is, and turn our lives around and follow Him. We shouldn't wait until the end. We don't know how much time we have to get things—spiritually and physically—in order. We might have only a few months, weeks, days, or even minutes. We can't tarry. Our first priority should be to get our spiritual house in order so we're ready to meet Jesus.

* * *

Jesus said the Holy Spirit will tell us things to come, and we can count on it as we learn to hear His voice and are open to His ways of communicating. In John 16:13, we read, "But when He, the Spirit of Truth (the Truth-giving

Spirit) comes, He will guide you into all the Truth (the whole, full Truth). For He will not speak His own message [on His own authority]; but He will tell whatever He hears [from the Father; He will give the message that has been given to Him], and He will announce and declare to you the things that are to come [that will happen in the future]."

So why does the Holy Spirit communicate with us? Simple. To keep us informed. That's just one of the many reasons the Holy Spirit communicates with us.

Dreams and visions are some of the ways the Holy Spirit speaks to us, to guide us through our lives. There are times these messages can be given to us to help someone else, as in the case of Mr. Smith. What troubles me the most about his passing is the uncertainty of whether or not he made it into heaven. My prayer is that he had received Christ at some point in his life, for Christ's mercy lasts forever.

To know God's voice we must first know Him. Jesus says, "I am the good shepherd; I know my sheep and my sheep know me" (John 10:14, NIV). The more we get to know our heavenly Father, the more we are able to distinguish His voice.

For those who believe God speaks directly to us in these modern times, He does so in multiple ways: His still small voice, dreams, impressions, and visions. Some claim that God doesn't speak directly to us. But He does; we just have to tune in. He can speak in the ways already mentioned, through the words of another, and of course, through Scripture.

Many people seem interested in the way God speaks through dreams. That explains the high level of interest in dream interpretation meetings, workshops, and books.

People have a strong desire to learn and understand what God is trying to reveal through their dreams.

That kind of knowledge carries great responsibility, however, and I wasn't happy with the way I handled it. I never directly asked Mr. Smith if he had a relationship with Jesus Christ. I have since learned it's better to be bold and obey the Holy Spirit when He gives such life-changing guidance. The Bible says it's much better to obey than to sacrifice (1 Sam. 15:22). I sacrificed to save the man's feelings—and also to save my job. In this country we are instructed to keep religious beliefs to ourselves, especially in the workplace. Because Mr. Smith became angry when I asked him about church, I stopped my questioning. I feared he might complain to management and have me fired. I try hard not to make that mistake again.

Since that time the Lord has given me many visions and dreams. In each one I learn something new and amazing.

CHAPTER 2

Comatose

But how are people to call upon Him Whom they
have not believed [in Whom they have no faith, on
Whom they have no reliance]? And how are they to
believe in Him [adhere to, trust in, and rely upon
Him] of Whom they have never heard? And how
are they to hear without a preacher?

—ROMANS 10:14

O NE AFTERNOON I walked into work at the For-
syth hospital with a sick feeling. I had signed up
for a twelve-hour shift and had been assigned to
the hardest unit in the hospital. I regretted volunteering
to work every step of the way to the elevator. I reached
the ninth floor and reluctantly asked the charge nurse
where the assignment board and report room were located.
When I gathered my assignment, I headed off to look for
the nurse from whom I would get my report.

When I caught up with her, she looked flat worn out. It
seemed not a single hair remained in place. Her eyes were
red and droopy. Her appearance confirmed that I was in
for a long, long day. She started describing the patients in
room numbers 9011 and 9012. I interrupted from time to
time to gather information I felt was essential in planning
my day of caring for the ten patients I had been assigned.

"In 9017 we have Mr. Johnson, who was admitted with
liver failure and severe ascites from long-term alcohol use.
He is unresponsive to any type of stimulation, and we
expected he would have already passed away days ago."

I prayed to overcome the fear that had slipped in while
hearing about this patient. "Please, Lord. Keep him alive
on my shift. I just can't do that today."

She continued, "He is a loner. He has not had any visitors since he was admitted a week ago. He listed a second
cousin as a contact person. The cousin lives three hours
away. We contacted the cousin and notified him of Mr.
Johnson's condition. He consented on the phone for Mr.
Johnson to be made DNR."

I finished gathering information for the remaining
patients and headed off for morning rounds. I approached
Mr. Johnson's room with great dread. He was a sor-
rowful sight to see. He lay motionless on the bed. His oily

dirty-blond hair was flat against his scalp with a four-plus pitting edema to every portion of his body but his face and neck. This means a nurse or doctor could press on the patient's flesh for several seconds and it would leave a very deep indentation, taking up to five seconds to return to its normal position. His face and neck were swollen but to a lesser degree. Trembling, I completed my assessment and thanked God that he was still breathing and had stable vital signs. As the nurse had said, Mr. Johnson was completely unresponsive to any stimulation. I had uncovered him to do my assessment, so I covered him back up and felt sad that he had no visitors to comfort him at the end of his life, which, based on his prognosis, could be today.

Throughout the day I checked on him at least once every hour. I wanted so badly to talk with someone who knew him to see what kind of life he had lived and if he had any spiritual beliefs. No one ever came.

Around 2:00 p.m., about seven hours after I started my shift, I decided I had to try something to reach out to Mr. Johnson. I knew he was going to die soon. Eight years into my career and at thirty-two years of age, I had never led anyone to the Lord because I didn't have the courage to pray out loud. But I decided I would give it a try with Mr. Johnson. I had heard other nurses say that hearing was the last to go. So I went to his room with the hope that his hearing was still intact. I leaned in close to him, feeling really weird about trying to pray with someone who wasn't responding to anything. Surprisingly I was calm. My voice never wavered. I didn't shake.

"Mr. Johnson, if you can hear me, I have to let you know that you are dying. I have been told that you should have died already. That's how serious your condition is. I just want to say that if you are not a Christian, I want to pray with you. Just repeat this prayer after me in your spirit. Jesus will hear you..." So I prayed the prayer, believing he was repeating it in his mind. Then I finished what I needed to do and left the room.

While I worked up discharge papers for two of my patients and admissions for two new patients, I wondered often about Mr. Johnson. Despite being tired from the hectic day, I continued to check on him each hour.

At 5:30 p.m. I began passing my last rounds of medications to my patients. I walked into Mr. Johnson's room to give his medications intravenously. As I slowly pushed the medication into his vein, a man walked into the room—Mr. Johnson's first visitor. I was pretty excited. Excited, number one, that he had lived and not passed away on my shift, and excited, number two, that someone was there to see him.

"Hi. Are you family?" I said as I continued to push on the plunger.

"No. We have worked together for the past fifteen years," he crossed over to the opposite side of the bed.

"Mr. Johnson, you have a visitor." I looked up at the man. "You can talk to him. He may be able to hear you. Do you know anything about him? Does he have family?"

I told this visitor I had been his nurse for the day and had tried to talk Mr. Johnson, although he was unresponsive. I put the needle in the mandated needle box as I talked.

"No. He doesn't have any family. He's always been a very quiet man. He mostly stays to himself," he said as he placed his hands into the pocket of his winter jacket.

"Do you know if he went to church?" I probed further.

"No. He didn't go to church."

"Do you?" I said, trying to determine if he ever talked with Mr. Johnson about God.

"Yes, I've been in church most of my life."

"Did you ever talk to him about Jesus?"

"No. We never talked about religion. I made sure I lived right in front of him."

So I told him I had prayed with Mr. Johnson even though I wasn't sure he had heard me. Then I finally said, "I'll leave you alone to visit him. Have a good night." And I left the room.

On my way out of the parking lot that evening I sat at the stoplight thinking about Mr. Johnson and how sad the end of his life was.

I heard the Lord say, "Did you hear that?"

I said, "What, Lord?"

He said, "He said he never told him. He just lived his life right before him."

That was a revelation for me that day. We have to tell people about Jesus. No one can determine who we are by watching how we live. Most people live good lives. They don't intentionally hurt others, don't steal, monitor their language, and go to work faithfully day after day. But there is no way for a person to know who believes in Jesus and who doesn't just by working with them or hanging out with them. Without our communicating with others and telling them Jesus loves them, those in our lives will never know who Jesus is and what He has done for us. That was a pivotal point in my life. I started speaking up after that and offering people the opportunity to hear. I honestly must say everyone I talked with from that point on was more than willing to hear about the love of God.

CHAPTER 3

Moses

For it is through Him that we both [whether far off or
near] now have an introduction (access) by
one [Holy] Spirit to the Father [so that we
are able to approach Him].
—EPHESIANS 2:18

UNNY THINGS HAPPEN in the workplace, and I don't mean practical jokes and the like. Although a good practical joke does relieve a little stress if the recipient has a good sense of humor, I'm not one for practical jokes. They really annoy me. Being a nurse, I really don't have time, and a health care environment is not usually the place to pull pranks. Those of us in this field need to stay focused on what we're doing, not be busy playing jokes on one another.

Now with that being said, a funny thing happened to me a few years ago at work. For the first time in my nearly ten years as a nurse, I cared for a patient named Moses. To some that might not be funny or even ironic, but to me it was. In my naiveté I didn't know anyone had ever named their child Moses. I really thought the only Moses ever to walk the earth was the man we find in the Old Testament. After I received the report from the night shift nurse, I was eager to go and see who this Moses was.

With my hair up in its normal ponytail, I entered his room through the glass door of the isolated room armed with my nursing accessories (scissors, pens of various colors, Critical Care Pocket Guide, alcohol swabs, Band-Aids, and anything else I could stuff in my pocket that might be of use at a moment's notice). My stethoscope bounced lazily against my chest. The blue curtain was pulled all of the way across the room blocking my view. I kindly warned, "Good morning. My name is Liz, and I'll be taking care of you today," as I pulled back the curtain.

Moses looked up, his eyes full of pain and hurt. Although he lay on the bed under the sheets, I could tell he was tall with a muscular body.

I tried to lighten his mood. "You are the first person

I have ever met named Moses! What made your family name you Moses?"

He grinned a little and said, "My mama."

"How awesome to be called 'a deliverer' from birth! Tell me about yourself." I continued to assess his health status as we talked.

Reluctant to talk at first about his personal life, he did finally open up enough for me to learn he lived with friends most of the time and had a sister whom he saw from time to time.

I had learned from the report that he was a long-time alcoholic and was in end-stage liver and heart failure. He was only in his forties. He didn't look like anyone who was near the end of his life. I'm sure this weighed heavily on his mind.

When I completed my assessment, I let him know I would be back to check on him in a few minutes. As I left the room, his breakfast was delivered.

I grieved for the man who carried a powerful name but was dying from alcoholism. I determined I would give him more opportunity to talk about his life and what he hoped to accomplish with the little time he had left. I checked on him quite often that day. Each time we talked a little, and the walls came down a little bit more.

Eventually we were able to talk about his hopes. Like all patients in his condition, he wanted to live a little while longer. I could sense there was more, but at that point his primary concern was living longer, and that's all he shared with me. It's sad to see people near the end of their life with regrets. Unfortunately we see this a lot. Many people realize they didn't do something they should have or have simply devoted their time and energy to things they thought were important but really weren't.

When we talked about his spiritual walk, Moses admitted he believed there was a God and he believed in Jesus. But he didn't feel he could approach Him. How many times have we heard this story before? People are afraid to approach our Lord and Savior because they feel they are not worthy. We are valuable to God, so valuable Jesus died for our sins so we can be worthy. That concept is hard for many to comprehend.

We also see this mentality in people who think they need to get their lives in order before they will attend church. This is backward. We should come to Christ for help getting our lives back in order, not wait to get it in order and then approach Him.

As Moses and I talked various times that day, I encouraged him that with a name like his, God had something planned for his life. I believe a name does define the potential in a person. I shared my feelings numerous times about the significance of a name. He seemed surprised that he could be anybody of any value. This is common among long-time drug addicts and alcoholics.

Sometime during the second day of caring for Moses and because of much conversation about God, Moses finally decided he wanted to have a personal relationship with Jesus. Just as Moses finished his prayer to the Lord, a man—probably in his late thirties or early forties—entered the room. He said he was walking by the room and felt the need to come in.

I said excitedly, "Moses just asked Jesus to be his Lord!"

I thought the man was a member of Moses's family, but it turns out he was a pastor. When he introduced himself, I realized none of us knew one another. We all looked at one another with a stunned look on our faces. After a brief moment of things being awkward, the pastor, satisfied that he had walked in on what God drew him in there for, said "Praise God!" and left the room.

The lesson that came to mind in dealing with Moses is that God always has a backup plan. Because of free will we may not follow the path planned for our lives. More than likely we've strayed a time or two. So God switches to the backup plan.

Who's to say that Moses should have given his life to the Lord years before he finally did? He may have had the opportunity, possibly numerous times, but chose instead to run from the Lord, either intentionally or unintentionally. Either way Moses made the commitment that day.

He recovered and was discharged, something I never thought would happen. Most patients in his condition never recover.

About three weeks later I came into the unit for a report. Moses was back. It concerned me because I automatically thought he had went back to his old ways. I was wrong.

We spoke briefly. He was back for medication adjustments. He had not started drinking again and *had* started telling his family he had given his life to Jesus. He had moved in with a family member who went to church. He was much happier. There was a glow of hope about him he didn't have during the first hospital stay. He was there only a day or two for med adjustments and was discharged home. I never saw him again after that.

CHAPTER 4

Doug's Revenge

Yet you do not know [the least thing] about what
may happen tomorrow. What is the nature of
your life? You are [really] but a wisp of
vapor (a puff of smoke, a mist) that is
visible for a little while and then
disappears [into thin air].

—JAMES 4:14

A FEW YEARS BACK I was assigned a patient with a disease I had never heard of—necrotizing fasciitis. When I started my shift that morning, the reporting nurse told me that this particular disease was deadly and its victims rarely lived. Necrotizing fasciitis, commonly known as flesh-eating disease or flesh-eating bacteria syndrome, is a rare infection of the deeper layers of skin and subcutaneous tissues. It spreads easily across the fascial plane within the subcutaneous tissue.

I've mentioned before that being a nurse can be tough and some afflictions are tougher to deal with than others. This one, for me, was the toughest. I saw and experienced things I hope I never endure again. As I cared for this patient, whom we'll call Doug, I probably felt like throwing up more times than I care to remember.

Doctors normally treat necrotizing fasciitis with surgery based on a high index of suspicion determined by the patient's signs and symptoms. The surgical removal of the infected tissue is the only treatment available for necrotizing fasciitis and is always necessary to keep the disease from spreading. Doctors confirm diagnosis by visual examination of the tissues and by tissue samples sent for microscopic evaluation.

Early medical treatment is often presumptive. Initial treatment often includes a combination of intravenous antibiotics that include penicillin, vancomycin, and clindamycin. Cultures are taken to determine appropriate antibiotic coverage, and antibiotics may be changed when culture results are obtained.

Amputation of the affected limb may be necessary. Exploratory surgery usually needs to be done to remove additional necrotic tissue, which often requires skin grafts because of the large open wound. Most patients require monitoring in an intensive care unit.

Despite the quick lesson I wasn't sure what to expect when I entered my new patient's room. His chart said he was fifty-three years old. I had often cared for patients that age, so as I approached his room, I didn't think much about it—until I saw him. He looked like an eighty-year-old.

Not only had he been diagnosed with necrotizing fasciitis, but he also was an uncontrolled diabetic. This meant he had difficulty maintaining reasonable levels of blood sugar to help his body fight off any sicknesses appropriately, let alone a flesh-eating disorder/infection.

As I approached Doug and introduced myself, I followed my usual assessment routines, including taking a blood sugar reading before his breakfast arrived. It was high, so I knew he would need some of the short-acting insulin the physician had ordered in addition to his regular long-acting insulin dose. We discussed how he was feeling and the plan for the day—pain medications, dressing changes, and so on. His breakfast came while I was in the room, so I excused myself to check on my other patient. My other patient was a burn victim. His dressings needed to be changed, and I knew that would take at least an hour. In a special care unit like this one, we have only two patients to care for each day. The patients have a lot of needs, and the intensity is too great for a nurse to care for more than two patients at a time.

Later in the morning I went in to change Doug's dressings. He needed this done three times a day, each lasting about thirty minutes. Not realizing what lay ahead, I assembled all my supplies and medications in an upbeat, cordial mood. We engaged in small talk as I set out to do my job. As I removed the bandages from his thighs, I realized the flesh-eating disease had not stopped there. I had to unroll bandages from his entire groin area too.

I had never seen anything so hideous. I had to look away for a few seconds to keep from losing the contents of my stomach. Thankfully the protective mask I wore hid my expression. I recomposed myself quickly and got back to work. The sooner I could finish, the better.

Every bit of flesh and underlying fat tissue was gone. Completely gone. A wave of nausea washed over me. This could have been an autopsy case. I could see entire muscles, tendons, and the fine layers that covered the muscles and tendons. I could even see testicles. (Yes, they are really white.) Up until this moment I'd been exposed to such things only in textbook pictures. Seeing something so grotesque up close really does test a person's resolve.

To mask my horror I asked Doug how his problem had begun. He said he first noticed a small, painful pimple on his inner thigh. After a few days he went to the doctor, who didn't seem concerned. However, the pain persisted and spread. The next thing he knew, doctors admitted him to the hospital and scheduled him for immediate surgery. That's how he landed in our unit.

Because he had a difficult personality, many of the nurses avoided him. They soon recognized that I got along with him, so I could always count on having him as my patient when I came in for duty. That didn't bother me. I made it my mission to show him someone cared. Doug admitted one day that the only family he had was his debilitated mother. One day a week she got someone to take her to visit her only son. No other family or friends ever came to visit. This type of situation tears at my heart. Being confined to a bed for any length of time is hard on a person physically, mentally, and emotionally.

Because I was the nurse who cared for him most, we had many opportunities to talk. During one of our discussions, he admitted his long-time drug abuse. He said he rarely used alcohol but did use and sell drugs. This information shocked me. I couldn't fathom someone his age living that type of lifestyle, but apparently drug users and dealers were his only circle of friends and business associates.

It didn't take long to realize I needed to share the love of Christ with him. I started talking to him about the forgiveness Jesus offers us and that He has a better plan for our lives. Despite being immersed in the drug world, he revealed that he believed in Jesus and a higher power, but he just wasn't ready to ask Him into his life.

I didn't want to push, a crucial element when sharing with people who have this mind-set. He and I spent some time every day discussing spiritual things in the midst of his suffering from the flesh-eating disease. I never pressed him to make a decision, but I did make sure that he knew as much about Jesus as I could tell him.

One day I finally asked him what kept him from coming to Christ. He said he had a score to settle with a man who had bought drugs from him but never paid for them. He wanted to get out of the hospital, get his vengeance, and then—only then—would he consider getting into church and receiving Christ.

Vengeance seemed like an unusual motivation for getting better. I knew he had little or no chance of leaving the hospital alive. He didn't realize how little time he had, and I didn't have the heart to tell him. So I kept encouraging him to let Jesus take his vengeance away. Each time I brought it up, he scoffed and said he would take care of business when he got better.

About three weeks into his stay, the charge nurse was

pressed for a bed for a critically ill patient. We decided to transfer Doug to a step-down unit adjacent to ours. Frustrated by having to move Doug, I held on to the hope that he would leave the hospital and have more time to consider his relationship with Christ.

A few days later I had some time off and was awakened one night by a brief vision. In it I saw Doug walking toward me dressed in his pale blue hospital gown. He looked calm and full of peace—not the expression I was accustomed to seeing. Normally Doug was uptight and angry because of his illness and the progression of the terrible disease.

In this vision I could hear his thoughts. He had only one thing to tell me: "Pride kept me from letting you pray with me." Then he disappeared.

When I awoke, I wondered what the vision meant and what I should do with the information. I believed the images and words came from God. He had given me information I needed for another talk. And I couldn't wait to get back to work the next day and check on Doug.

Around midmorning, after I had caught up with all my patients, I went to the adjacent unit where we had moved him. To my surprise he wasn't there. I wondered if he could have improved enough to be discharged. Or perhaps the hospital had sent him home because he didn't have insurance and hospital stays aren't cheap. I also knew dressings weren't cheap, and he needed them changed frequently.

Dismayed and confused, I returned to my unit and decided to take a quick morning break. One of our certified nurse assistants (CNA) took her break at the same time, so we chatted for a few minutes. I couldn't get Doug off my mind, so I finally asked the CNA if she knew anything about him. To my surprise she did. His condition had worsened drastically a couple of nights before and they had to readmit him to the unit. As they worked to settle him in the new room, he asked the CNA to call for the hospital chaplain.

She said the chaplain came and prayed with him to accept Jesus. Since she was also a believer, they all rejoiced. Later that night Doug died.

At that moment I realized why God gave me such a clear vision of Doug. He knew I was carrying a burden for Doug's soul and praying to find a way to reach him before it was too late. In His mercy He let me see Doug in his spirit and understand why he hadn't responded to my witness. God is so gracious.

Doug taught me an important spiritual lesson: both pride and vengeance are deadly. Psalm 10:4 says, "The wicked one in the pride of his countenance will not seek, inquire for, and yearn for God; all his thoughts are that there is no God [so He never punishes]."

These two deadly poisons can keep us from entering into the kingdom of heaven. But nothing is worth missing the goodness of God. We all will go through hard times. We all experience betrayal. The Bible says nothing on earth is new to mankind (Eccles. 1:9). We all experience events and circumstances we don't anticipate. Those who fail to seek the will of God will, from their own understanding, do things to hurt those around them.

Doug allowed his pride and vengeance to keep him from following Jesus. And Satan will hinder us from following Jesus too. Zechariah 3:1 says, "Then [the guiding angel] showed me Joshua the high priest standing before the Angel of the Lord, and Satan standing at Joshua's right hand to be his adversary and to accuse him." In 1 Thessalonians 2:18 Paul tells the Thessalonians that he wanted to go to them, but Satan hindered and impeded him.

* * *

Our human nature causes most of us to put things off. How many times do we wait until the last minute to wash clothes, buy groceries, pay the bills, or whatever task we need to complete? Our procrastination adds unnecessary stress to our lives and often to the lives of those around us—family, friends, or coworkers.

When it comes to life and death, though, any of us could be gone in a heartbeat. We need to consider our personal salvation ahead of time. And we must if we want to feel Jesus cup His loving hands around our face the moment we take our last breath. We must take time to ponder our destination. As the Bible says, "The simpleton believes every word he hears, but the prudent man looks and considers well where he is going" (Prov. 14:15).

My husband, Tim, asked me once what *prudent* meant, and I found an answer in Proverbs 16:21, "The wise in heart are called prudent," and in Proverbs 14:18, "The prudent are crowned with knowledge."

In the same way that we are birthed into this world as human beings, we will one day be birthed into the spiritual world as spiritual beings. Whether we believe it or not, we all will cross into another realm when we die. Like heaven, hell is forever.

Therefore we must be ready and consider, often with much thought and prayer, what is to come. May we cautiously avoid a simple mind, for the simpleton will go into outer darkness without a chance to reconsider what he once could have done something about.

Our heavenly Father wants to open our eyes so we will turn from Satan's darkness to God's light, from the grip of

Satan to the power of God. When we do this, we receive forgiveness, are released from our sins, and obtain our place in the kingdom of heaven (Acts 26:18).

When we choose to let go of those things that hinder us from releasing and receiving this forgiveness, God will lead us into a happier, more peaceful life here on the earth as well as in eternity.

CHAPTER 5

Huge Reptile

For I know the thoughts and plans that I have for
you, says the Lord, thoughts and plans for
welfare and peace and not for evil, to give
you hope in your final outcome.

—JEREMIAH 29:11

O NE DAY ON assignment to make a home care visit, I had one of the most terrifying experiences of my life. My patient was an elderly gentleman who lived in an upscale country club home outside Tanglewood Park in Clemmons, North Carolina. The little girl in me had longed to see inside one of the mansions in this neighborhood. So you can understand my disappointment when I pulled into the driveway of what looked like a typical ranch-style home. The front yard didn't contain a blade of grass, only vines. As I shifted the car into park I thought, "Vines. Looks like a snake den."

I parked the car, gathered all my equipment, and headed toward the front door. I introduced myself and, despite my disappointment, set out to complete my task quickly. This should have been an easy assignment. I only had to ask several questions to assess for problems; take the man's blood pressure, pulse, and temperature; and evaluate his respirations. Then I would look at his current medications and check for new ones. We always have to reconcile medications. According to government policy nurses have to confirm the old medications against any new to make sure what's no longer being taken or what's been added. Documenting it is part of the responsibility as we assess for problems with medications.

I'd finish up by making sure he understood why he was taking what he was taking and answering any questions he or his wife had. Both said they understood everything and were doing fine.

So far this seemed like just another routine field assignment. I chatted with the man and woman of the house while I tended to his needs. It didn't take me long to complete my task, probably about an hour. After giving both instructions of what to do next (give the doctor a call for any sudden changes or any emergencies and give our home care company a call for any questions or concerns), I was ready to head out the door. Before leaving, the home care nurse always has to have the patient sign a form verifying the visit to say the nurse came to the home for personal medical care.

My patient signed the paperwork. Then his wife walked me to the front door to say our good-byes. Holding my bag, I navigated carefully down the steps to keep from falling headlong onto the walkway as I heard the door click shut behind me.

BAM!

What felt like a huge electrical charge surged through my shins and feet. I stopped. My legs tingled then became numb. The shock affected not only my lower extremities but also my mind. In that moment everything around me faded away until my eyes focused on one thing: a large snake stretched across the sidewalk.

I couldn't tell the full length of the beige diamondback snake because the back half disappeared into the mass of vines near the sidewalk. But the part I could see was huge, at least sixteen inches in diameter with a head that must have been five and a half inches wide. Head raised, it stared at me, its black eyes locked onto me.

I backed up the steps, careful to not fall forward into the huge reptile. Behind me the door swung open. I turned and ran into the house, barging past the sweet old lady who had just escorted me out.

"There's a huge snake across your sidewalk," I stammered and gestured in an attempt to show her the size of the snake. My arms shook as I held my home care bag in my right hand and motioned with my left. "It's the biggest snake I've ever seen."

"Other people have told me they've seen a big snake out there," she said with no visible change in demeanor.

I longed to blurt out, "Then why haven't you had something done about it? It's headed directly up under your house." Instead I chose to keep my mouth shut and get away as soon as I could.

I intended to tell my manager to send someone else to that house next time. I never wanted to return. At the same time I felt astonished by the way the electrical field protected me by keeping me from stepping on the snake. Still stunned, I knew God had done a great thing for me.

If it had not been for God's divine intervention, my next step would have been directly into the midsection of that horrendous snake. I'm sure it would have curled around me and devoured me for dinner. I don't think it would have had much trouble, as it seemed much longer than my height of five feet, four inches.

✳ ✳ ✳

How can I not thank God for His divine protection after the many times He has spared my life? He promises in Luke that He has given us power over deadly things of the earth. We read, "Behold! I have given you authority and power to trample upon serpents and scorpions, and [physical and mental strength and ability] over all the power that the enemy [possesses]; and nothing shall in any way harm you" (Luke 10:19).

Interestingly enough when I saw the snake, I never made a sound. I was too shocked to speak or even scream. Yet when I returned to the house, my patient's wife said she'd heard me scream, so she came back to the door. The Lord must have let her know she needed to get back to that door because I was in trouble and needed to get inside—fast.

That day and many times since, I realized that our divine provision is always on time—not a second too early, not a blink of an eye too late. We have the assurance of God's divine protection and the knowledge that He uses every method available to make sure His children are safe, even from dangerous reptiles.

Remember, God has holy angels stationed all around you. Jesus had angels there with Him that awful night in the Garden of Gethsemane, and they are there for you too.

> And there appeared to Him an angel from heaven, strengthening Him in spirit.
> —Luke 22:43

God places that vast army of angels there to look out for us, to help us, and to strengthen us. The strengthening occurs in the spirit first and then travels to the mind. We must also realize many of us give the devil and his legion much more credit than they deserve. The Bible says there are twice as many holy angels as there are demons. That's a two-to-one ratio. I don't know about you, but I like having that kind of advantage over the enemy.

CHAPTER 6

Highway 21

For You, O Lord, have made me glad by Your works;
at the deeds of Your hands I joyfully sing.
—PSALM 92:4

A LONG DRIVE HOME, particularly at night, after a family vacation can be tough. Tired parents often take turns behind the wheel while the kids sleep. In 1978 Becky Tomlin took over the last leg of her family's trip home from Florida, easing up Highway 21 in North Carolina toward Yadkinville. Her husband, Al, dozed in the passenger seat while their three daughters slept in a makeshift bed in the back of the family's twelve-passenger van.

All seemed well as Becky drove along this two-lane stretch of roller-coaster highway. The van headlights provided the only light. With very little traffic on the road Becky concentrated on eating the bag of barbeque pork rinds she had bought when she took over the driving near Columbia, South Carolina. Clipping along at ten miles an hour above the speed limit, Becky's thoughts drifted back to the week the family had just spent in Indialantic Beach, Florida—until she felt the presence of an angel in the space between her and Al.

Suddenly feeling an angel in the van didn't alarm her, although she knew the angel was to help, warn, or guide them. Becky put her bag of pork rinds on the dash, turned off the radio, slowed down to the speed limit of forty-five, and put both hands on the steering wheel.

Her husband suddenly woke. Dazed, he looked around in an effort to get his bearings. "What's wrong?" he asked.

Not sure how best to tell her husband about the angelic visitor, Becky opted instead to assure him that everything was fine and under control. "Go back to sleep," she said, patting him on the leg.

Like most men, he pressed the matter, so Becky said, "There's an angel sitting between us."

He responded by telling her to pull over and let him drive.

Guiding the van down a long grade, Becky reassured him again that with this angel's help, they would be OK and that she was ready for whatever might happen. "That is why this angel is here," she said.

Her faith helped Becky understand that Jesus had sent His beloved angel to guard and protect her family. She sensed a connection in her mind, heart, and soul. Peace filled her.

At the bottom of the hill Becky pressed down on the accelerator to maintain the van's speed up the hill. When she crested the hill, an eighteen-wheeler sat in her lane. All lights were out on the broken-down vehicle.

Becky's husband yelled, "Look out!"

She swerved left into the other lane, just missing the corner of the truck. Fortunately for Becky and her family, no cars were in the other lane. Becky caught a glimpse of the driver walking along his rig, road flares in hand.

Gasping, her husband asked, "Would you like for me to drive now?"

Becky knew if she had been driving at fifty-five miles per hour, driving with one hand and eating pigskins with the other, without her full attention on the road, she would have plowed right up under the back of the truck, killing her and her family.

She didn't want her husband to drive. She needed to finish the trip as she thought about how precious her daughters were and how much she loved them and her husband.

She said a silent prayer, thanking God for delivering them from what would have been a terrible tragedy. She knew it was not God's plan for them to die that night, and He had sent His angel to protect them. The angel left Becky with a warm feeling that all was well for now, that she and her family were protected by faith wrapped in God's abiding love.

CHAPTER 7

Aneurysm

Honor (esteem and value as precious) your
father and your mother—this is the first
commandment with a promise.
—EPHESIANS 6:2

Sandra was nine years old when she dreamed her daddy, Sanford, was hit in the back of the head and collapsed to the ground. Her family gathered around him as he lay on a bed with a number of machines keeping him alive. Sandra woke up crying. The dream had been so vivid. Sandra shared the dream with her mother the next morning and told her she felt something bad was going to happen.

Her mother, Virgie, said, "No, everything is going to be OK. You just had a bad dream."

Sandra accepted that conclusion and left to catch the school bus. Still upset about the dream when she arrived at school, Sandra cried through most of the morning. Needing to share with a trusted adult, Sandra told her teacher, Mrs. Norman.

"Is he sick?" Mrs. Norman asked.

"No, he's not sick."

"Well, if he's not sick, try to think of good things."

Sandra tried, but she couldn't shake the dream. She walked around in a daze until her teacher tried again to comfort her. That helped for a little while.

After school Sandra waited for her father to arrive home from work. As the minutes ticked by, her nervousness increased—until he walked through the front door. Sandra ran to him and leaped into his arms. That night she stayed near his side, not wanting to let him out of her sight. Just before bedtime she shared with him the dream.

"I'll be fine," he said. "It was just a dream. Quit worrying. I don't plan on going anywhere."

Those words comforted Sandra. While others had said nearly the same thing earlier in the day, she needed to hear the words from her daddy. Though she thought of the dream occasionally, she pushed away the bad thoughts by remembering what her father had said.

Three years later she found herself clinging to her daddy. She couldn't keep herself from being upset and crying each time she thought of him. She didn't want to let him get out of her sight, but he had to leave for work and she for school. A feeling of dread and loss overwhelmed her.

Sandra told her mom, "Something's going to happen to Daddy." Her heart ached.

"No, he's going to be fine, Sandra," her mother said, sending Sandra out the door to catch the school bus.

When Sandra got off the bus that day, her sister was waiting to pick her up and take her to the hospital. Sandra's dad had been taken to the hospital in critical condition. He had worked for the granite quarry for most of his life. He would even go to work sick, but it was different this day; he left with a severe headache and went home to rest.

A little while later the oldest son, Danny, walked by his parents' bedroom and heard what he thought was snoring. He thought that was odd because his dad never snored. He went in to check on his father and found him hemorrhaged out, blood surrounding his head. Because the family didn't have a phone in the house, Danny jumped into his car and drove two miles to the neighbor's house and called for an ambulance.

For three months Sandra's dad lay in a hospital bed in ICU hooked to a ventilator, IVs, various monitors, and a Foley catheter. A tube hung from his head to drain a disgusting brown fluid from his skull. He never regained consciousness.

He did respond with tears when Sandra would kiss or touch his face or her mother or sister would touch his arms and hands. As an adult now Sandra vividly remembers the first time she saw her father. The monitors and tubes shocked her. She cried. The doctor was speaking with her mother. She looked at her dad. Tears rolled down his cheeks. Up until this time her father had been a vibrant man. She took one of his hands into hers and cried some more.

He had left work early that day to come home and rest because he felt too sick to finish the day. Sandra couldn't remember her father ever leaving work, particularly because he was sick. He went home and crawled into bed in hopes of finding relief from the horrible pain.

The pain, doctors discovered, was from a brain aneurysm. He was placed on a respirator that kept him alive for three months.

The strain on Sandra's mom grew with each passing day. She was torn between caring for five children and being at the hospital as much as possible. Sandra's oldest brother and an uncle Curtis stepped in. They decided it was time to sign the papers to take Sandra's dad off life support. He was forty-seven when he died.

A few weeks later Sandra and her mom sat at the kitchen table, talking and eating snacks. At one point her mother said, "You know that was God's way of trying to let you know He was getting ready to take your dad home to heaven."

But the story didn't end there. Some time later, as Sandra continued to grieve her loss, she dreamed of her father. He said, "Don't cry. One day we will all be together again. Be strong for your mom." Sandra was happy to see her father again as they walked and talked.

Crying, Sandra woke and immediately told her mother about the dream. Her mother started to cry too.

"He's gone to heaven to get us a home ready so one day we can all be together again."

✳ ✳ ✳

Isn't it wonderful how God will give us the surety of knowing where our family members are when they die? God also wants us to know that we can have this same surety about our own eternal fate. This knowing will give us peace and hope when we face our own end-of-life circumstances or that of a close friend or family member. The Bible says:

> Brothers, we do not want you to…grieve like the rest of men, who have no hope. We believe that Jesus died and rose again and so we believe that God will bring with Jesus those who have fallen asleep in him. According to the Lord's own word, we tell you that we who are still alive, who are left till the coming of the Lord, will certainly not precede those who have fallen asleep. For the Lord himself will come down from heaven, with a loud command, with the voice of the archangel and with the trumpet call of God, and the dead in Christ will rise first. After that, we who are still alive and are left will be caught up together with them in the clouds to meet the Lord in the air. And so we will be with the Lord forever. Therefore encourage each other with these words.
> —1 Thessalonians 4:13–18, niv

CHAPTER 8

The Bear

Many plans are in a man's mind, but it is the Lord's
purpose for him that will stand.

—PROVERBS 19:21

In October 1997 my daddy was given only three months to live. The news shocked us. He was only sixty-four years old. How could he leave us at such a young age? I wanted more time with him—more time to build up our relationship.

I struggled with these questions as fall gave way to winter. Nothing—reading my Bible, praying, talking with my family, crying—brought me peace or comfort. The more I thought about his passing, the more my heart ached. I needed more time. I had lost so much time with him because we were a broken family. We didn't have a close relationship because our family split apart when I was eleven years old.

Like many who have faced the imminent passing of a parent, I couldn't imagine life without my father. If you've lost a parent, you know what I'm talking about. If you haven't, know that when your mother or father dies—regardless of how close you may or may not be today—your heartache will run deep.

In early December, a few months after Daddy's diagnosis, I dreamed I was walking across the flat, well-maintained lawn of his hundred-year-old house in southern Virginia. Tufts of green grass poked through patches of snow. Like a bad movie rolling through my mind, everything happened in slow motion.

As I neared the house, I tried to suppress my emotions so Daddy wouldn't see my pain. I took cautious, measured steps. We had only a few days left to spend together. I concentrated on taking slow, even breaths. I was sure anyone within three feet could hear my heart pounding. My arms and legs felt as if they each had a ten-pound weight attached.

I had walked to within five feet of the gray wraparound

porch when a black bear barreled across the yard from my right. I panicked. Instead of running into the safety of the house, I stopped. Unable to scream, I braced for the impending impact. Instead of knocking me down, the bear latched onto my right forearm with his teeth. I feared a mauling, but the bear only stood there, my arm in his mouth. I remained motionless but still couldn't scream. I was too afraid to breathe.

The mauling I feared never came. The bear did, however, keep me from entering my dad's home. While he stood there with my arm in his mouth, my sister Dorothy walked across the porch and entered through the front door, oblivious to both the bear and me.

This dream occurred two weeks prior to Daddy's passing on December 27. The night before his death, mentally and physically exhausted after thirty-six straight hours of caring for my daddy, I went to a nearby hotel for some much-needed rest around 7:00 p.m. I planned to get up early the following morning and return to pray and care for him.

After a heavy night's sleep, I awoke at 7:25 a.m. and promptly showered. After I dried off, I felt the urgent need to pray for Daddy's healing and knelt on the cold bathroom floor. A few minutes later a knock on the outside door interrupted my prayer.

I threw on some clothes and answered the door to find my brother and uncle. Through deep, heavy sobs, my brother told me Daddy passed away earlier that morning. We hugged and then sat on the edge of the bed where we hugged and cried some more.

A few days later when the shock of his death had waned only a little, I pondered the dream I had prior to his passing. Bears typically indicate death, which we knew was coming for Daddy. When I thought about all the events that led up to his entrance into eternal glory, I finally understood my dream. The bear holding me outside of the house meant I wasn't supposed to be inside the house when Daddy died. But my sister was. That's why she was able to enter the house unhindered.

The night after Daddy died, my mom awoke from a restless sleep and saw Jesus and my daddy standing in the room, talking. My parents had divorced many years before, but Daddy looked over to Momma and said, "I'm sorry for what I did to you."

They all smiled at each other, and Jesus and Daddy disappeared. Relieved to see Daddy with Jesus, my mom went back to sleep. She told me the next day about the encounter.

Daddy had also told my aunt Mamie that he would send a big snow when he got to heaven. On the day of his funeral it snowed about four inches. It was beautiful. While sitting in the funeral home, Aunt Mamie smiled and, with tears in her eyes, said, "Jay told me he was going to send us a big snow when he got to heaven." It made everyone in hearing distance laugh through their sobs.

Since childhood I have experienced the supernatural wonders of dreams and visions, though as a child I didn't understand what was happening. If I had written down these experiences and dreams when they started, I'd have enough notebooks to fill a small barn. As I grew older, I began to understand how personal God is. He is not a remote deity who sits on His throne and watches for every mistake we make. Nor is He harsh and unloving, as many unfortunately believe. God is always there—longing to communicate with us and wanting to reveal great mysteries of the spiritual realm.

If you wonder why He wants to spend time with us or

to know the smallest details of our lives, the answer is simple: He created us for that purpose. He longs for us to have a personal relationship—a friendship—with Him. And friendship only exists in relationship. That holds true in your relationship with your best friend, your spouse, or the Lord. Relationships are sustained only with ongoing communication.

The key to an ongoing relationship with the Lord is prayer. We can't pick up the phone to call Him, and we can't send Him an e-mail. We have to pray. The New King James Version of 1 Thessalonians 5:17 is comprised of just three words, three words that speak volumes of what God asks of us: "Pray without ceasing."

Have you ever written down a prayer or something the Lord said to you in your prayer time? Because we are told to pray without ceasing, it's not always possible to do that. Most people tend to jot down a note or two during their quiet time.

By praying without ceasing, we remain in constant communication with God. How many times have you had a friendship that ended because at some point the communication became a one-way street? True friends share and are always ready to go beyond themselves to help each other. Not only does our heavenly Father reveal His great love and mercy through the supernatural, but He also desires to overflow us with personal blessings—blessings that are far above anything we can imagine. And that comes forth from having and developing a long, loving relationship with Him.

Little did I know the dream about my daddy wouldn't be the only one about a family member. In December 2010 I had a dream about my cousin Frank, whom I loved like a brother, but I was tied up in knots for a while about whether or not to share. I wasn't looking to gain favor in his eyes. I knew the dream was a warning.

In my dream he vanished, and I knew I would never see him again. The pain was excruciating. A few days later I decided I should tell him. I wrote him a letter, explained the details, and encouraged him to live for Jesus because life is short. I told him I could handle never seeing him on earth again, but I couldn't handle knowing I would never see him again in eternity.

I mailed him the letter.

In response he sent back a letter that said, "Liz, life is short." He mentioned a few other things in the letter: that he missed his children (they lived in another state with their mother) and, "You have been preaching to me all my life, Liz."

Six months later I received a text from my husband, Tim, to inform me of Frank's death on May 5, 2011. The dream didn't lessen the pain I felt when I heard the news. Frank's passing was agonizing for our entire family.

I know the Lord knows our beginning, end, and all that is in between. He also knows our intentions. Kind of scary, isn't it? Like with Frank, God knew what was going to happen. So the Lord gave me a dream to help Frank take another look at his life and where he stood with God.

Another time a few years ago I was drawing closer to the Lord and asked Him to purge me of things in my life that were unhealthy spiritually and physically. On July 21, 1995, He opened a window in my soul. He gave me a night vision that urged me to seek Him earnestly for its meaning.

In the vision my oldest daughter, she was about four in the dream, and I were laughing and chatting as we walked to visit my dad. When we arrived, we sat down and noticed his brothers were somber and expressionless.

My dad seemed to be the focus. He was pacing around the group making incomprehensible sounds. We stopped laughing, and I asked, "What's wrong with him?"

No one answered. Dad's features suddenly became distorted, and he made a comment about my brother. As soon as the words left his mouth, a strange possession consumed me. A powerful presence of rage and anger filled me. I opened my mouth wide, and a ferocious, inhuman roar poured out. Its force was so strong I could feel my face flapping. I was terrified because I had no power to control it. Suddenly the words "Jesus, Jesus" sounded from somewhere in the depths of my mind—and I woke.

In the stillness of the night God can reveal hidden strongholds in our lives. He speaks this way because distractions stop when we sleep. In fact, sleep becomes a highway of communication between our spirits and the Spirit of God, and we connect to places we have long forgotten or never been before. We must also understand that Satan wants to deceive us, so he will come in a form of light through our dreams at times too. Again, we must test the spirits to see if they are of God (1 John 4:1).

The interpretation of this night vision changed my life. I was not aware of the anger and rage that had developed inside of me during my childhood toward my dad. I thought I just had an uncanny ability to forgive my parents' offenses, but in reality I had developed the ability to suppress the pain. Pushing emotions down is a common survival method among children who have been misused. Through our dreams God is able to reveal these suppressed feelings and start the healing process.

* * *

Even today I continue to seek God for healing from my past, and I have become a new person as a result. Am I perfectly made over? Of course not! I am still a work in progress, but I will not stop until everything is purged and I can live as the person I was meant to be in Christ.

Your defect may not be anger or rage. Maybe you lie, steal, cheat, fornicate, commit adultery, or gossip. The list of potential imperfections is endless. Whatever our weakness is, it is impossible to correct a problem we are not aware of or that we refuse to acknowledge. But our heavenly Father knows how to get our attention.

Take time, then, to evaluate your dreams and ask the Lord if they have meaning for your life. When He speaks, trust Him to help you deal with your need. Many great leaders say their success comes from spending time with successful people. And there is no better influence than the Holy Spirit of God. He is the Creator of success. Listen when He speaks, follow where He leads, and He will take you into the desires of your heart.

Ask God to reveal your inner intentions, to help you let go of the old ways and take on His ways. Only then—as you die to yourself and live to the Lord—will you have the opportunity to build successful relationships.

> A [self-confident] fool has no delight in understanding but only in revealing his personal opinions *and* himself.
>
> —Proverbs 18:2, emphasis added

> He who has a wayward *and* crooked mind finds
> no good, and he who has a willful *and* contrary
> tongue will fall into calamity.
> —Proverbs 17:20, emphasis added

Don't let old thought patterns steal your present joy. Ask God to purge you of corroded opinions of others and move you into worthwhile relationships. This takes plenty of patience—and practice.

I grew up in dysfunction, so I became a suspicious person. I thought I had a sixth sense and could read people well. The problem was I did not give people the opportunity to get to know me because I always thought they had ulterior motives. It took many years for me to recognize my true problem: a suspicious mind. When I experienced freedom from its grip, I knew I never wanted it back.

Reading the Bible and understanding what the Holy Spirit was saying to me about my character led me into freedom. We all can have that same kind of freedom. We won't get it in every area of our life. The freedom comes in stages, little by little, step by step. The more we read and listen, the more refined we become, and the easier it will be to recognize a warning from the Holy Spirit.

CHAPTER 9

Yes, Lord

In the reverent and worshipful fear of the Lord there
is strong confidence, and His children shall
always have a place of refuge.
—PROVERBS 14:26

Living in a small town like Yadkinville, North Carolina, has its advantages. Most people know each other. People very seldom lock their doors, and children ride their bicycles on the streets without the worry of being kidnapped.

Nursing runs in the Tomlin family, so it was no surprise when at age sixteen Rebecca started her career as a nurses' aide at the sixty-bed Lula Conrad Hoots Memorial. She went on to receive her degree as a licensed practical nurse from Guilford Technical Community College. Soon after graduation she returned to Hoots.

One day a man in his mid-eighties, Mr. Collins, was brought into the emergency room after being found unresponsive by his son. The emergency room doctor determined that Mr. Collins's diabetes was out of control and he needed to be admitted. He was a frail-looking man with a meek spirit. He was so humble and had that special sparkle in his eyes. Nurses and doctors fell in love with him immediately.

A week into his stay the sparkle in Mr. Collins's eyes disappeared when his son decided to put him in a nursing home. That answered the question a number of nurses had about whether or not Mr. Collins would get strong enough to go home and take care of himself. During that week in the hospital Mr. Collins, like many patients, had some good days and some bad days. There were days that he was so weak nurses had to help him turn over in the bed.

A few more days had passed by, and the nurse on first shift was reporting off to Rebecca. She had reported that Mr. Collins had a good day. He was more alert and had sat up in the chair for a few hours. She was excited for him and thought that maybe his health was turning around.

That evening on the hall was very busy with admissions,

labs, assessing patients, and getting medications out to them before 4:00 p.m. Supper was to be served an hour later, so Rebecca had plenty of time to distribute her medicines. She entered the four-bed ward of room sixty-three. The patients in the room were ambulatory except for Mr. Collins. Because of that Rebecca gave Mr. Collins his medicine last so that she could take more time to assist him. That day he appeared more alert and was not sleeping as usual. Instead he stared at the ceiling.

As Rebecca approached him, putting his medicine down on his nightstand and proceeding to pour some fresh water in his cup, she asked, "Mr. Collins, how are you?" She paused then said, "I have your medicine."

He didn't acknowledge her and continued to stare intensely at the ceiling. Then he said, "Yes, Lord, I see You now."

Rebecca took a closer look at the ceiling but didn't see anything. She then tried to get his attention again by touching his shoulder. "Mr. Collins, can you take your medicine for me?"

As he looked at her, slightly agitated, she placed the pills in his mouth and gave him water. Mr. Collins swallowed and redirected his gaze toward the ceiling.

Finished with him, she left the room only to hear him say, "Lord, just please do not make it hard on them."

Rebecca returned to the nurse's station after distributing her medicines, wondering what was going on with Mr. Collins. "He has never acted this way before," she thought. A few more minutes had passed when a nurses' aide came running up to the desk.

"Something is wrong with Mr. Collins. I think he is gone," she said.

With the aide following her, Rebecca ran down the

hall and turned into his room. When she reached his bed, he wasn't breathing. The duo started CPR and continued until the doctor arrived and pronounced his time of death.

While they waited for Mr. Collins's son to arrive at the hospital, Rebecca replayed the scenario from earlier. She realized Mr. Collins was in the presence of the Lord when she interrupted him to take a pill that now seemed trivial. She could hear him saying again in her head, "Yes, Lord, I see You now." and "Lord, just don't make it hard on them."

A joyful feeling came over Rebecca at the realization that Mr. Collins was with Jesus and the angels in heaven. She knew that he was having a conversation with God and she had interrupted them. She also knew he no longer suffered and was now with loved ones who had gone on before him.

When Mr. Collins's son arrived at the hospital, he spoke with the doctor. Rebecca found him standing at his dad's bedside trying to understand and realize that his dad had passed.

Rebecca placed her hand on his shoulder and told him about the conversation his dad had earlier that evening with God and his angels and how she felt that they had come to take him to his heavenly home.

She also told him what an inspiration his dad was in his faith and how his dad lifted and strengthened her heart. Rebecca could feel the weight lift from his shoulders, and he agreed that he knew that his dad was in a better place. He seemed comforted again to be reminded of his dad's love and that the angels had taken him home.

✳ ✳ ✳

Many people have reported their loved ones seeing and describing angels during the transition from life to death. Angels help guide us into God's holy presence when our work on earth is done. We see an account of this in the Gospel of Luke when Jesus gives a description of Lazarus's death. In Luke 16:19-22 we read:

> There was a certain rich man who [habitually] clothed himself in purple and fine linen and reveled and feasted and made merry in splendor every day. And at his gate there was [carelessly] dropped down and left a certain utterly destitute man named Lazarus, [reduced to begging alms and] covered with [ulcerated] sores. He [eagerly] desired to be satisfied with what fell from the rich man's table; moreover, the dogs even came and licked his sores. And it occurred that the man [reduced to] begging died and was carried by the angels to Abraham's bosom.

We in the medical profession sometimes have the privilege of sharing in sweet moments like this. We feel the person who has just died must have seen either an angel or Jesus as they passed from this world to the next.

These are tender, touching experiences. They provide a grieving family with a precious gift: the comfort of knowing for certain where their loved one will spend eternity.

In some ways, nurses are like angels. They care for those in need, often during their darkest hours. In fact, a nurse's goal must be to care for the patients' needs and to make them as comfortable as possible during their time of recovery or passing.

In a similar way, our Father sends the angels to care for mankind. He assigns angels to help us with every need, to make us as comfortable as possible as we face times of trial and testing, and to usher us into God's presence when our time on the earth is done.

CHAPTER 10

Z-28

For he shall give his angels charge over
thee, to keep thee in all thy ways.
—PSALM 91:11, KJV

A N ACCIDENT ONE cold October evening changed Dean's life forever. A free spirit, he cruised around town in his compact economy car. That night he pulled away from an intersection into the path of a speedy Z-28. Dean later learned the driver of the car was going well over one hundred miles an hour in an attempt to outrun the state patrol.

Dean's little car buckled in half. The impact knocked Dean unconscious. When he came to, he discovered the transmission housing and gear shifter pushed up to the roofline of the car, the doorposts driven through the doors, and the bucket seats snapped off at the base. The engine from the Z-28 sat in the middle of the intersection. He struggled to move and, despite three years of nurses' training, was oblivious of possible injuries. He simply wanted to get out of his mangled car. Working his way out of the broken seat, he crawled slowly through broken glass out through the hatchback of his beloved car. Finally free of the car, he stood and his legs buckled, sending a searing pain through his head and neck.

He grabbed his head, the pain more intense than any-thing he had ever felt. He rolled over numerous times— through shattered glass and liquids leaking from both cars—until he reached the side of the road. The smell of gas and burnt rubber hung like a thick fog over the scene. A hissing sound emanated from one of the cars.

Dean literally had to pick up his head with his hands to lay it on the curb. Despite the pain, he began a self-analysis of his injuries. He diagnosed a possible neck fracture, a damaged or severed spinal cord, and possibly leaking spinal fluids. Any one of these injuries could be lead to paralysis. All three together pretty much assured that fate. His fingers tingled, another bad sign.

Dean looked up into the nighttime sky; the stars shone, and the cold air brought some relief to his broken body. This was a good night to die, he thought. He worried how his parents might take the news. And then something stranger than fiction happened: the stars disappeared and his life began to play out before his eyes.

As a child Dean often played with an 8mm camera. The movie in his mind looked like that. Each scene was a small vignette; each part of his life played out as he lay there on the cold pavement awaiting help. He relived the comments and actions he made to people, both good and bad. He felt their pleasure. And worse yet, their pain. He saw missed opportunities, chances to help others that he had passed up.

All this happened within a matter of seconds. Dean didn't pause to think how cliché this was or about how others had described the same type event having happened to them. When the visions stopped, Dean realized the "good" life he thought he lived had not been so perfect after all. He cried and asked for forgiveness for his sins and those of "omission." Believing he was close to death, he asked God to give him a chance to live a better life.

God, it seemed, answered that prayer immediately. A large authoritarian figure approached and spoke to Dean, "Let's get you out of this road before someone else runs over you."

Dean couldn't see the man's face, just a glow from the headlights of vehicles that had stopped to help. The man scooped up Dean, offering support with massive arms, and laid him in the back of a patrol car. Despite the chaos and numerous people on the scene, Dean was the only one who saw this person.

Medics soon arrived and ran an initial check on Dean.

He was loaded into the ambulance and taken to the local hospital. Initial X-rays revealed major cervical fractures front and rear. Still in unbelievable pain Dean was strapped to a board and taken to a trauma center about thirty miles away. There further tests were administered. Dr. Cortland Davis, one of the best neurosurgeons on the east coast and since retired, was assigned to Dean's case. He told Dean's family that he had a 90 percent chance of not making it through the night. Cervical bones were shattered in the front and rear of Dean's neck, some near the axis of C1 and C2. Farther down there was apparent damage as far down as C5 and C6 in the rear of his neck. Bones were crushed, making them irreparable. Dr. Davis said that *if* Dean made it through the night, there was, again, a 90 percent probability he would be paralyzed and wheelchair-bound the remainder of his life.

Things were moving quickly now. They injected Dean with Demerol and Valium, and he remembers the warmth flowing from his left arm, across his chest, and into his right arm. A set of tongs was then attached to Dean's skull similar, if not exactly, to Mayfield tongs. This entailed drilling and insertion of the screws into Dean's skull while he was conscious. Dean remembers screaming as the doctor on one side and the assisting nurse on the other screwed these devices into his skull simultaneously with a T handle. Later Dean's head was put in ten pounds of traction. He threw up from the nausea.

The next four days were filled with periods of awakening to excruciating pain, injections, and unconsciousness. His parents never left his side. His church was notified and began prayer vigils. During this time a war was being waged that no one knew about. On one side evil was trying to convince Dean that this was a "God act." "God has done this to you—the God you actually tried to serve."

Dean's pastor at the time asked him what he had done so wrong to deserve the constant battle in his mind. Replays of scenes of his life again dominated his mind's eye. Only this time the scenes were of temptations he had resisted. This time the enemy said, "I would have given you this and more, and now look at you. You can't even move!"

In his sedated stupor Dean asked God for an answer. The answer was simple: "Trust in Me."

By the end of the fourth day he told God that it wasn't enough. The images of a relentless enemy were offset by God's few words of "trust in Me." Dean wanted more than that. Early one day about 2:00 a.m. Dean tried to get up and leave while still in traction. He had to be restrained by the nurse on duty as she lay across his bed to prevent more damage being done by his actions. Dean was tired—tired of the battle, tired of God's answers, and tired of being taunted by the enemy. Most of this time, due to the sedation, he was not even able to pray for himself, but others did. And thank God, they did.

A lady near where Dean lived got word of his predicament. She was an older lady, a Pentecostal preacher. She said she was sitting on the couch and God spoke to her and told her to go see Dean at the hospital. She could have just sat there that cold day and said, "God, You can touch him from here. I'll just stay here on this comfortable couch and pray for him," but she didn't. She had her daughter load her up in the car and drive the thirty miles south to pay Dean a personal visit, just as God had instructed.

Dean cried out often because of the pain. When he did, the nurses injected him with Demerol or Valium. At that point it didn't matter which. Whatever drug they administered knocked him out like a light. One afternoon, however, he suddenly awoke. He recognized a woman's voice, but he couldn't turn his head to see his visitor. He also felt another presence in the room—and in his body.

It felt like every cell of his being was about to explode. The lady walked over to his bed and reached through the rails to hold his hand.

"I've been praying for you," she said.

Tears streamed down Dean's face. "I know," he said, aware of something odd happening in his body. "I want you to pray with me now."

She then prayed. Nothing stood out in the prayer as being magical or moving. Dean noted the serious tone of the words she spoke, words more serious than he had ever heard in his life.

As he closed his eyes, he could see himself suddenly standing vertical. Something warm, with the consistency of oil, traveled down his head and through his neck into his chest and the rest of his body. Healing was taking place. And Dean knew it. Of course, the enemy tried to discount it.

Later that day Dr. Davis made his daily check on Dean. Throughout Dean's explanation of what had happened just that day, modern science only recognized what they saw and understood. They didn't understand or recognize miracles. There was no need for more tests, the doctor said.

One of the reasons, the doctor explained, that they had left Dean lying for four days was because, quite frankly, they didn't know what to do with him. Bones were shattered with no means for repair. He wanted to do exploratory surgery the next day, commenting, "We don't expect to find any repairable materials. We fully expect you to be wheelchair-bound with tongs intact the next six months here in the hospital, and maybe after that, you can go home where you'll have to remain wheelchair-bound the rest of your life. You'll have to take it easy that you don't have additional fractures that would cause breathing or autonomic nervous system impairment."

The prayers were still going up. Dean knew what he felt had happened, but he agreed to the surgery. If God is God, after all, He can stand one of His children being examined after a miracle, he believed, had occurred.

The operation was over. Dean was back in his room. The earlier prognosis was that he would have to wear the tongs indefinitely. As he regained consciousness, Dean immediately noticed his head no longer hurt. He reached up, still with his eyes closed, and smiled as he discovered the tongs formerly in his skull were gone. He continued to feel around his face and neck to discover that he wore only a lightweight whiplash collar.

Tears began to flow. His mother appeared and was crying as well. "It's so wonderful, Dean," she said. "Those tongs are gone."

As the tears of joy continued to fall, the family waited for the doctor to come give his report. Dr. Davis soon entered the room, somewhat downtrodden. Three others in long white coats joined the doctor, who Dean later learned was an atheist.

Dr. Davis stared at the floor as he spoke, "Dean, some things in life we just don't understand. When we got in there, we found only superficial injuries. You are free to get up when you feel like it, and we'll have you out of here soon." He then turned and left the room.

Get up? Walk? Go home?

Just a few short hours earlier Dean's destiny was a wheelchair. Now he could go home? The celebration in the room could hardly be contained. The next couple of days Dr. Davis sent several interns and assistants into Dean's room for inquiry into exactly what happened. Each was told the story of a miraculous healing. Nurses sent in others from down the hall with the same type injuries. Dean witnessed to an heiress of the R. J. Reynolds estate who herself was a victim as he was. Spiritual doors opened, and Dean walked through every one of them. No more omissions.

Why did God heal this old country boy? Dean still doesn't know, except that He loves Dean just as He loves you. Dean still doesn't understand why good people still suffer and die, but he's long since stopped trying to understand. All he knows is something God shared with him later on: "There is only love, and there is only now. If you feel impressed to do something good, do it now. Don't wait. Share God's love today."

CHAPTER 11

A Little Boy, a Grandpa, and Jesus

Truly I say to you, whoever does not accept and
receive and welcome the kingdom of God like a little
child [does] shall not in any way enter it [at all].

—LUKE 18:17

NTHONY, A TEN-YEAR-OLD diagnosed with an incurable liver disease, spent the final moments of his life in a hospital bed surrounded by family and medical personnel. His nurse Sheri stood by his side on the opposite side from his mother.

His care was palliative at this point, meaning comfort measures only. Because of various setbacks Anthony didn't receive the treatment he needed when he needed it. Anthony's quality of life could have been good for many years or he could have gone into remission, if he had had proper medical care. Because of situations in his family his medical care had been delayed, and now it was too late to reverse the damage to his liver

Now they stood watching, waiting for the heartbreaking last breath.

Tears streamed down Sheri's flushed face as she ensured his oxygen was securely snuggled beneath his nose. She brushed her hand gently across his cool forehead and down his cheek as his little body became lifeless.

Anthony's mother held a tissue to her nose and ran her fingers through his soft hair with her free hand. She struggled to speak. "It's OK, Anthony. I'm here."

Other members of the family fought back their own tears. Some sniffled. Some held tight to each other.

Doctors and nurses, tears in their eyes as well, stood at the ready.

Anthony gasped, quieting the room. He looked up into his mother's eyes.

As Sheri's heart raced, she wished she could do more than be an authentic presence. She focused on the family. This was it—Anthony's last raspy breaths. In three years since graduating from nursing school, this day had become one of the hardest of her career.

"This hurts too much. Anthony is such a sweet boy. This just isn't fair. He's too young. If only they could have taken him to the doctor earlier," she thought.

Sheri took a deep breath and held back the tears.

Anthony's eyes moved from his mother's to off in the distance. He smiled. "Momma, I see Jesus."

He relaxed. The gasping stopped as he released his final breath.

An eerie silence settled over the room for a moment. No one breathed. No one moved until Anthony's mother collapsed onto her son's little chest. She held his lifeless body tight for the last time. The sniffles returned. Tears flowed. Heavy sobs filled the air that a moment ago hung in silence.

Sheri thought, "We can't always know why things happen as they do, but one thing is for sure; when a child dies, it brings out the humanity in us all and the grace of God."

Despite the knowledge that earlier treatment might have prolonged Anthony's life, or even saved it, his family can take comfort knowing he walked from the loving arms of his family into the loving arms of Jesus.

✳ ✳ ✳

Everyone who believes (adheres to, trusts, and relies on the fact) that Jesus is the Christ (the Messiah) is a born-again child of God; and everyone who loves the Father also loves the one born of Him (His offspring).

—1 John 5:1

Like most six-year-old boys Jonathan loved his great-grandpa. He spent many days visiting his mom's grand-father. He'd sit on the floor and play, often listening to well-told stories about the store his great-grandfather had owned.

Things soon changed one spring. The visits became more frequent. Great-Grandpa didn't have as much energy as before. When he pushed his five-foot-five frame up from the favorite recliner where he always sat, he didn't move as well as before. His white hair was thinning, and his skin was tanned from many years of working outside on his farm. He shuffled instead of walked. But he always wore a suit. And he still laughed a lot.

One particular day in the middle of a conversation, the look in Great-Grandpa's blue eyes changed. Jonathan watched as his great-grandfather stared off into the distance and smiled.

"Grandpa, what do you see?" Jonathan's mother asked.

"I see angels," he replied.

Unlike most six-year-olds, Jonathan wasn't unnerved. His great-grandfather had modeled Christ in both actions and words. He often spoke of Jesus to his great-grandson. Jonathan knew angels were God's helpers.

When this happened a second time, Jonathan knew, because of family conversations, that Great-Grandpa wouldn't live much longer. He didn't understand that cancer was eating away at his great-grandfather's lungs, but he understood that Great-Grandpa would soon live without pain or suffering.

✳ ✳ ✳

Real-life experiences like this often inspire people to seek more of our heavenly Father. Adam and Eve enjoyed God's companionship in the Garden of Eden. God desires to have a close relationship with us now. Sin separates us from God, but Jesus Christ restored that relationship through the blood He shed on the cross. We can walk with God when we receive Jesus into our hearts and the Holy Spirit of God indwells us. This gives us a divine connection to the supernatural.

And who knows? Maybe someday we'll see Him escort a dear friend or family member into heaven.

CHAPTER 12

Four-Year-Old
and an Angel

And now, little children, abide (live, remain
permanently) in Him, so that when He is made
visible, we may have and enjoy perfect confidence
(boldness, assurance) and not be ashamed and
shrink from Him at His coming.

—1 JOHN 2:28

O NE COLD WINTER night in 2004 Nick woke up to the smell of smoke. Intense heat filled the master bedroom, the air too thick to inhale.

Reaching over to his wife, he tried to rouse her as he screamed, "Kalei! Do you smell smoke?"

As his wife forced herself to wake, "Yeah, I do! We better get out of here!"

Nick tried to stay calm while he and his wife covered their faces and felt their way out of the bedroom. Their two young children slept in separate bedrooms at the opposite end of the mobile home.

They could feel the intensity of the heat pouring from the flames as they groped their way through the living room, past the kitchen, and into the entrance to the hallway. Nick knew it was impossible to get through the hallway to save the kids. He turned back to Kalei in a panic and yelled above the crackling of the flames, "Get out of the house!"

Kalei shot back, pointing down the hallway. "But Nick, the kids!"

Kalei welled up with tears. Her babies were down that hallway. Nick grabbed her and forced her outside onto the front lawn. Dressed in only a lightweight nightgown, the winter air cooled the outside of her body. Inside, a fire of its own raged. She needed to get to her boys. Later she discovered she had sustained extensive burns.

Flames poured from every window of their mobile home. As she struggled to catch her breath, the entire structure engulfed in flames was almost too hot to even look at.

Nick ran along the side of the single-wide mobile home looking for a place to enter. He took a chance through a door on the porch. Inside, he fumbled for the knob of the kids' bedroom door. He could hear the kids crying and found his boys clinging to each other inside one of the bedrooms. Both boys were covered in a thick black layer of smoke. Choking on the acrid heaviness, Nick forced his way out with both boys, one under each arm. Their skin was badly burned and their pajamas had melted to their skin.

With flames burning away their clothes, Nick dropped the boys on the lawn. Kalei screamed, "Oh my God! Konnor and Kameron!"

Nick collapsed to the ground in a heap. He had sustained life-ending injuries from the flames. As this realization fell on Kalei, she screamed "Nick! Oh, God!"

"I've saved the kids, Kalei, but I'm not going to make it," he gasped.

"No, no. You're going to be all right. You're going to make it through this…."

Nick died that horrible night. Kalei, Konnor, and Kameron were transported to a nearby trauma center.

Four-year-old Konner and his two-year-old brother, Kameron, were placed in the pediatric intensive care unit. Kalei was sent to an adult intensive care unit. Konnor suffered severe burns to his face, neck, chest, and both hands. His therapy included pressure garments to his hands in an attempt to minimize the scarring. This was done to try to protect his joints and attempt to give him some sort of functioning hands once he healed. The staff, however, felt he would never be able to use his hands again.

Despite his young age Konnor was a compliant patient. He let the nurses and doctors do whatever needed to be done without complaining. His psychological and social health was waning. His affect was somber, and he suffered with nightmares nightly. He was having a very difficult time adjusting not only to the changes in his body but also to how alone he was. With his mother and brother still being treated for burns themselves, he was alone most of the time except for medical staff. A child psychologist was finally called to consult with Konnor.

After a month of these difficulties one night nurse, Tabatha, was caring for Konnor. She noticed that he wasn't fretting through the night as he typically did. She checked on him many times through the night and each time Konnor was sleeping like a baby. He was so peaceful she was tempted to turn off the monitors connected to him, but she knew she couldn't do that.

As she was preparing to leave the next morning, Konnor woke up.

"Hey, sleepy eyes. You sure slept good last night. What was different?"

Konnor blinked his beautiful blue eyes. The dressings covering his face and neck left his eyes to express emotion. "A man came and sat down with me last night. He held my hand all night long."

Nurse Tabatha didn't know what to say to Konnor, but she mustered a few words. "Really? Well, he sure did a good job because you slept the best I have ever seen." She lightly tapped him on the shoulder as she said, "See you tonight, little guy. I love you."

CHAPTER 13

RSVP

Are not the angels all ministering spirits (servants)
sent out in the service [of God for the assistance] of
those who are to inherit salvation?
—HEBREWS 1:14

S ANDRA PICKED UP her six-month-old son, Andie, from day care at 5:00 p.m. one Thursday in March. She noticed right away that he wasn't his typical perky self. His skin felt hot, and he coughed from deep within his chest. The congestion sounded horrible. Being a nurses' assistant, Sandra thought he might have an upper respiratory tract infection.

Concerned, she strapped him in his car seat and headed home. Upon their arrival she bathed him and put him in his crib for the night. She and her husband checked on him throughout the night, often wiping his runny nose. Thankfully his symptoms never worsened.

In the morning Sandra readied herself for work and Andie for the day-care center. At 2:00 p.m. Sandra received a call from her husband that the day care had called to inform him that Andie's temperature had shot up.

Sandra met her husband at home to help take care of their baby. That night, with Andie's temp still high, they decided to take him to the emergency room. A quick diagnosis indicated that Andie had a virus, but he would be OK. Sandra and her husband breathed the proverbial sigh of relief. They took Andie home to recover.

Early the next morning Sandra entered the nursery to change Andie, who was wheezing and crowing, hoarse breathing sounds that indicate respiratory distress. Her husband called the doctor, who advised them to get Andie back to the emergency room, where he would meet them. This time an X-ray of Andie's chest was taken. The doctor discovered that Andie suffered from a relatively new affliction, respiratory syncytial virus.

The doctor immediately ordered transport to a nearby children's hospital, a larger facility better suited to treat patients with Andie's ailment. Andie was strapped to a gurney with Sandra strapped in against him at his side. A non-rebreather mask, used to increase oxygen intake, was placed over his face. Sandra fought back tears as she watched and prayed for her baby.

When settled into a semiprivate room at the hospital, Andie was given fluids and more oxygen. His condition seemed to stabilize. But two hours later, around midnight, the alarm on his machine went off. Nurses ran in. One pushed Sandra aside to attend to Andie. Another nurse soon asked Sandra to step outside.

"He's very sick and has gone into respiratory arrest," the nurse said before giving Sandra directions to the waiting room.

Sandra wandered down the hall, unsure of what might happen to her child. She and her husband alternated between sitting and pacing. They prayed, cried, and prayed some more.

During a moment of sitting, a ten-year-old boy waiting with his grandfather walked up to Sandra and put his arm around her. "Lady, don't cry. There are angels all around your baby. Your little boy is not going to die."

His grandpa said, "Come here. You don't need to be over there bothering them."

"Oh, he is no bother," Sandra said. Crying, she reached out and hugged the boy. "Thank you so much. Thank you so much."

The boy, waiting for news about his ailing sister, then hugged Sandra's husband. "Everything is going to be OK," he said. Then he smiled and walked back and sat in the seat next to his grandfather.

After perhaps the loneliest thirty minutes of Sandra's life, Dr. James entered the waiting room. Sandra and her husband braced themselves for the news. Smiling, he sat next to Sandra and her husband. "A miracle has happened. Everything is going to be OK," he said. "Your son is going to be OK. You can come back in the room and hold your baby."

"Now?" Sandra asked.

"Yes, now."

Sandra and her husband followed the doctor back to Andie's room. Sandra leaned over and held her son in the tiny bed, crying. "Thank You, God." Then to the doctor, she said, "If you weren't a believer, this would change your whole outlook. It would make you a believer in God."

"Obviously there is a God in heaven," Dr. James said as he turned to walk out of the room.

At the time many children died within twenty-four hours of respiratory syncytial virus. Andie remained in the hospital only another fifteen hours. While sitting next to her son in his hospital bed, Sandra often thought of the words from the little boy in the waiting room. "Lady, don't cry. There are angels all around your baby. Your little boy is not going to die." And then she'd cry and thank the Lord again for His healing power.

CHAPTER 14

Angels in the Room

The Angel of the Lord encamps around those who
fear Him [who revere and worship Him with awe] and
each of them He delivers.

—PSALM 34:7

SOME TIME AGO a friend of mine, Christy, had to deal with the pain of her eighty-year-old grandmother's diagnosis of liver cancer. This was Grandmother Marie's second fight with the dreaded "c" word. Nine months earlier she had been diagnosed with skin cancer of the face that metastasized to her neck and lymph nodes.

The grandmother's husband died eleven years earlier, and she had never recovered from her loneliness. Her loving family surrounded her, but to her nothing could replace the companionship of her soul mate.

She had been receiving chemotherapy for nine months but decided she no longer wanted to endure it. Within a week after stopping treatment, the sure signs of death began to appear.

For several days she diminished into a mysterious world of her own as she became less and less aware of her surroundings. In her final twenty-four hours she was completely unresponsive to family and friends who gathered in her bedroom. Dressed in white cotton pajamas with pink flowers, she lay sweetly nestled in the soft sheets and blankets, surrounded by pictures of her husband.

In her final moments her longtime friend Dot leaned in close. Marie opened her eyes for the first time in twenty-four hours and looked up to the sky. She moved her mouth as if to share something amazing as she raised her hands. Unable to speak, she turned her gaze back to her friend. Within moments she was gone.

As the people in the room witnessed these events, everything came to a halting silence. Tears streamed down their faces, and whispered sounds of "Praise God. Amen" came from all sides.

✳ ✳ ✳

I also had an experience with a patient who saw angels while I tended to her in her hospital room 1011. In 1995 Lacy Brown and I hit it off right away. While we try to build a rapport with the patients and their families, it doesn't always happen. But Lacy and I got along right from the start.

Lacy was a frail, black, seventy-six-year-old widow. Doctors admitted her to the cardiac step-down unit with exacerbated congestive heart failure. This condition causes fluid to back up into the lungs and, if not treated, ultimately drowns the patient. When a patient is in this state, they are put on oxygen, usually with a flow rate of two liters per minute, and given Lasix (a fluid pill) twice a day and Lanoxin, which helps the heart pump blood out with more force. We also have to keep their head elevated and monitor their oxygen saturation levels every four hours.

A pleasant and friendly lady, Lacy made conversation easy. We laughed most of the two days I cared for her, although, sadly, I was the only company she had. None of her family lived nearby, and most of her friends had already taken their trip into eternity. To say we developed a special bond is an understatement. There was something about Lacy that made it easy to talk with and spend time with her. I found myself thinking of her often during the day, although I had nine other patients to care for both days.

At the end of the second day, as I finished my shift rounds, I entered Lacy's room. I deliberately made her my last stop so I would end work on a happy note. But that didn't happen. She complained she was having difficulty breathing. As she tried to explain her condition, she struggled more to breathe. I listened carefully while I elevated the head of the bed and assessed the situation.

I asked, "Has this ever happened to you before?"

She gasped, "Oh yes, honey. It happens to me at home sometimes…" She couldn't finish her sentence.

Within minutes her oxygen levels had fallen and her heart rate increased. I could hear the congestion in her lungs as she struggled for breath, so I made sure that her supplemental oxygen was working adequately and called for help.

"Ms. Brown is short of breath, her lungs have crackles bilaterally in all fields, her oxygen levels are falling, and her heart rate is increasing. I need you to notify her heart doctor immediately," I anxiously reported to the charge nurse.

As I completed my routine checklist, I realized her respiratory status was rapidly worsening. Despite this she had a sparkling glow in her eyes. She also was having a conversation—but no longer with me.

I anxiously asked, "Ms. Brown, who are you talking to?"

More than anything else I wanted to get her to hear me so I could stall her impending respiratory arrest. This act of desperation came because I was alone in the room with her and could perform only limited treatment without orders from her medical doctor.

Slowly she lifted her brown bony finger and pointed directly ahead of her. "I'm talking to them angels crossing the river."

I think my heart missed a beat or two. I was really torn about whether or not to stop her from going with the angels. I didn't want to stop her from meeting Jesus and her eternal destiny. At the same time I was trained to save lives, not lose them.

Her condition quickly deteriorated, and her limited oxygen supply would no longer sustain her life. The help I'd requested finally arrived, and we paralyzed her with Pavulon (a muscle relaxant commonly used to aid intubation) while a respiratory therapist put a breathing tube down her trachea and hooked her to a breathing machine. After stabilizing her, we transferred her to the cardiac care unit.

When I returned to my own unit, I got back to work finishing up final care of my remaining patients. I had gotten to the end of the hall preparing to go into the patient's room with the prescribed medications when my beeper went off. With a sigh I looked down and read, "Patient in room 1011 SOB."

SOB is medical language for "short of breath." I did a double take when I realized which room. I thought they must be mistaken because I had just transferred Lacy to her new unit, so I continued with my current task. Less than a minute later the beeper went off again: "1011 SOB."

Figuring this was a mistake, I decided I'd check to see what the secretary was talking about. I walked into the room and saw a woman lying in the bed. But it wasn't Lacy. While I transferred Lacy, the charge nurse had moved a patient into the room without telling me. I walked to the side of the bed without knowing anything about this woman's condition, diagnosis, name, or anything and asked, "Are you having trouble breathing?"

Her reply was hard to hear. Then she stopped breathing! I looked up to see an internist walking into the room. I looked back down at the new patient and said to the internist, "She's not breathing!"

The internist grabbed one of the patient's wrists. "She doesn't have a pulse!"

"Here we go again," I thought. "Another code in the same room just minutes after Lacy coded." We put the woman on a ventilator and got a heart rhythm back after administering a number of intravenous medications to get her to that point. Then we transferred her to the same unit Lacy had been transferred.

Needless to say, I seriously considered leaving the nursing profession that night. I was relieved to go home at the end of my shift.

Two days later I came back on shift, anxious to see what had happened to Lacy. To my surprise I found out she had lived, been transferred to a general floor, and was on her way home. I immediately made my way to see her. Unfortunately the other woman did die.

When I entered the room, I asked, "Do you remember me?"

She smiled and said, "Yes."

I smiled back as I looked around her room. Lacy was fully dressed and stretched out on the bed as she waited for a ride home. The heart monitor hung silently on the wall. The tubing for the oxygen was wrapped around the base attached to the wall. The IV pole with half-filled bags of fluid were disconnected and stuffed into the far corner.

"Do you remember what happened the other day before you were taken to the cardiac care unit?" I quizzed.

With a sweet grin she replied, "No."

Then I asked if she had a relationship with God.

Her smile widened. Her eyes glistened. "Oh yes, honey! I'm in the church every time the doors are opened."

Then I told her about the angels and that she had quite a testimony to take back to her church. She raised her hands, laughed, and praised the Lord!

It warmed my heart to see her so happy. We laughed together. A few minutes later, when I left to get back to my own unit, Lacy was still praising God.

We all have days in which we enjoy our work more than other days. That morning with Lacy was one of those. I wish all my hours at the hospital could be like that. I would dance into work every day. After that day I never saw Lacy again, but I will never forget her and the angels.

Imagine for a moment life without angels. Maybe the automobile accident would have claimed your life? Or the drug overdose? Or something else catastrophic, such as a hurricane, flood, or tornado?

God put those angels around us to keep us safe. He loves us and wants to give us all the assistance we need to successfully complete our purpose in life.

We are never alone.

CHAPTER 15

Jesus in the Ambulance

I am the Alpha and the Omega, *the Beginning and
the End*, says the Lord God, He Who is and
Who was and Who is to come, the
Almighty (the Ruler of all).
—REVELATIONS 1:8, EMPHASIS ADDED

THE CALL FOR an ambulance came in around 9:00 p.m. Audrey left her three teenage sons at home and headed out the door to meet another medic at the ambulance bay for the volunteer department. When she arrived, they jumped into the ambulance. In a matter of minutes they rolled onto the scene in a rural area of southwest Pennsylvania.

Nothing seemed out of the ordinary when they entered the home. The petite patient, who suffered from cancer, struggled to breathe and was in a lot of pain, all indicated during the call for help. The woman's daughter, a nurse, had started an IV. Audrey administered oxygen and made final preparations for the customary "scoop and run." Six minutes after arriving, Audrey and her crew headed down the driveway toward the hospital thirty-five minutes away.

While her friend drove through the winding rural roads to the hospital in Morgantown, West Virginia, Audrey administered more drugs to help ease the patient's pain. The two chatted, including a few moments about the patient's grandson and Audrey's youngest son being teammates on an elementary school basketball team. Fifteen minutes from the hospital, the patient abruptly ended her conversation with Audrey.

A moment later the patient raised a steady but weak right hand and stared at something at the back of the ambulance. Then she spoke.

"I see you. Yes, I'm ready."

"Who are you talking to?" Audrey asked, turning toward the back of the ambulance.

The patient didn't answer, but instead she continued the conversation with the unseen person. She repeated over and over for nearly five minutes, "I'm ready. Yes, I'm ready. I see you. I'm ready."

As the conversation continued, Audrey tied a brace under the patient's right arm to help keep it raised.

The other medic, who chose to ride up front, and the driver weren't aware of what was happening in the back. Audrey could hear bits of their conversation in between the patient talking to her unseen friend.

About five minutes from the hospital, the conversation with the unseen person stopped. The patient closed her eyes and then opened them again. "Audrey, we're almost to the hospital. Will you please fix my babushka?"

Audrey wondered how the patient knew they were close to their destination. It was dark out with no late summer stars in the sky.

"Are you OK," Audrey asked.

"Yes, I'm fine."

Emergency room personnel had a room waiting for the patient when the ambulance arrived. Audrey and the other medic wheeled the patient into the room and left. The next day a member from the patient's family called to thank Audrey and to inform her that the woman died ten minutes after being dropped off at the hospital, a little after 10:00 p.m.

Thirty years later Audrey still remembers the serene feeling in the back of the ambulance. She sensed another presence at the time. Up until that incident, despite being a believer, Audrey didn't believe dying people had those kinds of experiences. She'd heard and witnessed people saying such things as "Jesus is over there in the corner" or "I see an angel in that corner." But she blamed it on heavy medication. However, she knew this patient, and she wasn't drugged up that night in the ambulance.

"That's something you don't forget," she said recently. To this day she still cries when she talks about the experience.

CHAPTER 16

Cole and Jesus

We love Him, because He first loved us.

—1 JOHN 4:19

Ο NE HOT SUNDAY evening late in the summer of 2010, eight-year-old Julia stood at the windowsill of her brother's bedroom and watched Jesus escort her six-year-old neighbor Cole to heaven. Earlier that day the boy lost a two-year battle with cancer. His passing devastated family, church members, and friends around the country who followed the updates on his deteriorating health on social networking sites, including one devoted to him.

After Cole's diagnosis at age four, the disease slowly took its toll on his body. By April 2010 he could no longer walk or move his arms. By the middle of July he couldn't open his eyes or mouth. And for the final six weeks of his life Cole lay in bed, unable to communicate with those around him. They could do nothing but watch as his life slipped slowly away. He passed a little after 4:00 in the afternoon.

Although his passing came as no surprise, it certainly didn't diminish the family's crushing grief. Losing a child hurts. Burying one as young as Cole numbs the soul.

Julia's experience of watching Cole take his eternal walk into heaven provided peace and comfort for those who loved the little boy. A little over an hour after he passed, Julia and some friends were playing in her younger brother's bedroom. Without saying anything to the other children, she took a break and walked to the window.

As she looked out over the yard, she saw things many people here on earth have never seen. A cloud, lined with lights and jewels that sparkled from the rays of the early-evening sun, descended from heaven. But the cloud's passengers overshadowed its beauty. Little Cole stood there holding hands with a man in a long, flowing robe. Right away Julia recognized the man as Jesus.

Like many who have seen Jesus—or angels or demons—she just knew. They didn't need a neon sign or a one-hundred-foot billboard. "You just know," they say. "You just know."

Julia knew. She smiled as Cole turned and waved. Then Jesus turned and waved too. Her smile broadened.

She no longer cared about her friends or the game she had left. Instead Julia stared wide-eyed at the splendor of Jesus in His golden robe. He stood tall, about the height of one of her middle-aged neighbors.

And Cole? Julia told her mother that Cole's face glowed and his smile spread wide. "He looked happy for the first time in years, smiling, laughing, loving life like he did before he got sick," she said.

A large number of angels—more than Julia could count—surrounded Jesus and Cole. Some waved palm branches as Jesus passed by. Some sang "Starry Night." Others simply waved their hands in the air. She noticed one angel played guitar. All were smiling.

Jesus continued to smile as He said, "Julia, you should tell your mom, and you should tell other people too. You should tell everyone. You should tell them I love them a lot."

Jesus's long brown hair flowed onto His shoulders, touching the red sash that hung from His left shoulder and tapered diagonally to His waist. It partially covered the jeweled buttons on the front of His robe. Jewels also lined the edges of this golden robe. A pair of silver sandals—also decorated in jewels—covered His feet.

For his ascension into heaven Cole wore a silver robe encrusted with jewels on the sash and hem and a pair of silver sandals also decorated in jewels. On his right arm he sported the multicolored Silly Bandz popular with children and some teenagers. Cole and Jesus each wore a belt adorned with dazzling jewels.

A few days later, when Julia finally told her mother about her experience, Julia said the robes "looked soft and cozy and warm."

She also said that as Cole and Jesus rose in the sky, they "were smiling and waving at me."

Some of the angels stood like statues, guarding the fence around the property of Julia's home. Mesmerized, she watched as Cole and Jesus moved through the singing angels of various sizes, all with bejeweled wings. Julia, who had seen angels before, was fascinated nonetheless by the large, medium, and small angels, each with long wings that protruded from their backs.

According to Julia, the little angels (those around five to six feet tall with wings twelve to fourteen feet wide) could fit into the home she shared with her mom, dad, and brother. Some of the middle-sized angels also could fit into the house. But the angels that surrounded Jesus and Cole were much larger. With feet firmly planted on the ground, each rose far into the sky, their heads touching the heavens. The wingspan of these angels stretched nearly twenty feet wide, enough to fill their family room at its widest point.

Some of the angels wore silver robes with gold sashes across the chest; others wore plain gold robes. All wore silver sandals lined with jewels. The belts (similar to those worn by martial artists) cinched around their waists were covered with jewels—some shaped like stars, others like arrowheads.

To celebrate the joyous occasion, the angels sang as they watched Jesus and Cole rising into the sky in escalator-like fashion on a giant sparkling cloud. Seven points and swirlies, like the clouds described in Ezekiel, lined the edge of the cloud. The constantly changing colors reminded Julia of Christmas lights.

In Ezekiel 1:4 we read, "As I looked, behold, a stormy wind came out of the north, and a great cloud with a fire enveloping it and flashing continually; a brightness was about it and out of the midst of it there seemed to glow amber metal, out of the midst of the fire."

We find another reference to a vision like this nine chapters later in Ezekiel 10:1–2: "Then I looked and behold, in the firmament that was over the heads of the cherubim there appeared above them something looking like a sapphire stone, in form resembling a throne. And [the Lord] spoke to the man clothed in linen and said, Go in among the whirling wheels under the cherubim; fill your hands with coals of fire from between the cherubim and scatter them over the city. And he went in before my eyes."

Still on the cloud of many colors, Jesus and Cole continued to smile and talk. They stopped and waved again to Julia. Excited, she waved back as they ascended above the trees. Then she was pulled away from the vision by her friend Kasey asking a question. Julia turned to answer, and when she returned her gaze to the backyard, Cole and Jesus were both gone.

Right away Julia tried to tell her mother, Rebecca, about the vision, just as Jesus had instructed. But her mother was busy working out details for the lemonade stand Julia's entrepreneurial six-year-old brother wanted to build so he could take the profits to buy land on which to build a restaurant. When Julia finally shared the story a few days later, her mother recalls that Julia was "so excited, but wasn't jumping up and down" like one might expect of a child her age.

At one point Julia told her mother, "Jesus told me to tell you." Since then the two have retold the story dozens, possibly hundreds, of times. It should come as no surprise that people love hearing about Julia's experience. Her story brings hope, encouragement, and relief.

CHAPTER 17

Twisted Car

Thank [God] in everything [no matter what the
circumstances may be, be thankful and give thanks],
for this is the will of God for you [who are] in Christ
Jesus [the Revealer and Mediator of that will].

—1 THESSALONIANS 5:18

ONE FRIDAY SUMMER day in 2011 Sandra received a troubling phone call from her son Andrew, who was about to return home from a quick trip to Washington DC.

"Mom," he said. "Let Grandma know that I will take her if she needs to go anywhere."

"Why?" Sandra said.

"I called her last night to let her know I'd be there today to eat fried chicken with her."

He then dropped in something that shook Sandra. "I dreamed last night that someone in the family passed away."

"Oh, son, it's just a dream," she said while worry crept in.

Throughout the day, during breaks from her nursing job, Sandra called her mother, Virgie, several times to make sure she was OK. Sandra began to worry when her mother never answered. After numerous unanswered calls, Sandra called her brother Danny at the service station next door.

"Oh, she's fine," her brother said. "She went to run errands. She'll be back in a little bit. Don't worry about her."

Sandra then went back to work. While cleaning up a patient's room, she felt nauseated from a piercing open vision—flashes of a car twisted in half. She couldn't see who was in the car or even recognize the car. She braced herself, wondering if this had something to do with her son's return trip from Washington DC.

She couldn't see who was involved in the accident but felt she needed to go home. She walked out of the room and talked with the charge nurse.

"I just don't feel right. I think I just need to go home," she said. "I just saw a car twisted in half flash before my eyes."

"No, you can't go home," the charge nurse said. "Just go take your break. Everything will be all right."

Another nurse standing nearby chimed in, "Aw, Sandra, everything is all right. Don't leave."

An hour later Sandra was summoned to the nurse's desk for a phone call.

John, her husband, was on the other end, "Sheri, your mom has been in a bad wreck. She's been airlifted to Baptist. Punch out. I'll come get you, and we will ride down there together."

Her mind suddenly fuzzy, Sandra told the charge nurse, "I have to leave." Then Sandra quickly filled her in on what John had said.

The charge nurse's mouth dropped open. "Well, I am so sorry. Is somebody going to come and get you?"

"Yes, I am going to have to leave," Sandra said with a distant voice.

"I hope everything is going to be OK."

Sandra punched out and went outside to wait for her husband, her thoughts on the vision and her mother. She hoped the two weren't connected, but she knew they were.

She doesn't remember much of the ride to the hospital, other than a lot of crying and shaking uncontrollably. Sandra and her husband arrived at the hospital. Andrew, despite having car trouble, made it by 6:00 p.m.

At first doctors believed Virgie had a few broken bones and some controllable bleeding, but she needed surgery. Sandra signed the necessary papers. Soon the doctors discovered things were much worse than they thought.

After surgery Virgie was placed in ICU. Only two family members at a time were allowed to visit. Sandra's husband and Andrew went first. Sandra braced herself. She feared the worst and tried to hope for the best.

Andrew returned to the waiting room first. "Mom, you probably do not need to go back there."

After putting it off as long as she could, Sandra gathered the strength to see her mother. She wasn't prepared for what she saw: her mother swollen to three times her normal size and hooked to various machines to keep her alive.

Sandra stood next to the bed, fighting back tears. She talked to her mother. Rubbed her hand and said: "It's OK. We're all here together. If you feel like you need to go on and be with Dad, you go ahead."

When she ran out of words but with more tears needing to flow, Sandra returned to the waiting room to be with her family. The doctor soon joined them.

"We really need to make a decision. Her outcome is not good at this point," he said. "We don't know how much pain she is in."

He looked at the chart and recited some important information: O2 level at 75 percent, low blood pressure, low hemoglobin. Sandra knew the situation was grave. Her mother already had received ten units of blood. The decision to remove her mother from life support would not be an easy one, but it needed to be made quickly.

Five minutes after turning off the machines, Sandra's mother passed away.

She turned to her son. He said through tears, "I guess in that dream God was trying to tell me someone I loved dearly was going to pass away."

"I guess so," she said.

When Sandra later saw her mom's car, it was twisted in half, just as she saw in the vision.

* * *

God often gives us a cue to warn of impending danger. I wonder if we fully appreciate the way our heavenly Father often gives us this heads-up, or warning, of things to come.

In Scripture we see this in Job 33:14–18, "For God speaketh once, yea twice, yet man perceiveth it not. In a dream, in a vision of the night, when deep sleep falleth upon men, in slumberings upon the bed; then he openeth the ears of men, and sealeth their instruction, that he may withdraw man from his purpose, and hide pride from man. He keepeth back his soul from the pit, and his life from perishing by the sword" (KJV).

When God gives us a supernatural warning, we should stay close to Him and tuck under His protection so we're not enticed by any spells of the great illusionist Satan or the ways of his pesky demon subjects.

CHAPTER 18

Fiery Pit

Unto You do I cry, O Lᴏʀᴅ my Rock, be not deaf and
silent to me, lest, if You be silent to me, I become
like those going down to the pit [the grave].
—PSALM 28:1

FRIDAY, OCTOBER 28, 2005 is a day Matt Marion will never forget. That's the day he should have died. More accurately, he should have burned to death.

That night Matt, his wife, and two children were preparing for bed in their home in northern North Carolina when Matt became restless and decided to do some more work on their property. Earlier that day he had cleared some trees and brush as part of the final steps in building a massive fishing pond. He had been working on this project for several months and was almost to the point of filling it with water and eventually fish. He looked forward to many days of sitting on the shore with a fishing pole, his children nearby with poles of their own.

A country boy from Davie County, Matt was accustomed to working into the late hours of the night. He walked over to the sliding glass doors and called over his shoulder, "Melissa, I'm going to add some trees to the fire." He grabbed his flashlight and headed into the night.

He scurried outside to retrieve the borrowed Bobcat skid-steer tractor, an eight-thousand-pound machine encased with a cage on three sides. The driving compartment's sole entrance lay at the front. A neighbor had loaned Matt the tractor when he saw his diligence and the vast amount of land he had set out to clear.

Athletic and a top competitor in every sport he tried, Matt took great pride in completing any project he started. He hoped building this pond—despite it being a much longer task than he had anticipated—would prove to be a rewarding task.

Matt hoisted himself into the entrance in the front of the Bobcat, sat on the leather seat, and swiveled himself into position. He reached up to pull the safety bar down over his lap and turned the key into the "on" position. The motor purred as Matt pulled the tractor up the hill to gather his first load of logs and brush. With the skill of an expert he slid the bucket into the pile and lifted up his first scoop of the night. He maneuvered the Bobcat toward the fire, a huge pit six feet deep, ten feet long, and twenty feet wide. Little did he know that within a few more minutes this pit would threaten to become his grave.

After dumping several loads into the now-roaring fire, he noticed it was around 10:14 p.m. Like most hard workers, he wanted to get one more log on the fire before turning in for the night. This simple decision nearly cost him his life.

He decided to finish the night by grabbing a nearby ten-foot log, a task that proved more difficult than the others he'd completed that night. He lowered the bucket, scooped up the log, and lifted it high into the night sky before heading straight for the edge of the flaming pit. Without a second thought he positioned the tractor on the edge. To his surprise the weight of the bucket caused the Bobcat to lose its balance, teeter, and fall into the fire.

Trapped, Matt feverishly tried to maneuver the machine out of the pit. He jammed it into reverse, back into gear, and reverse. It wouldn't move. The back tires lifted off the ground and prevented him from gaining the traction he needed.

The heat from the fire was more intense than anything he had ever felt. Each breath he drew in made him feel as though knives were slicing down his windpipe and into his lungs.

Matt tried to stay calm. He knew clear thinking would be critical to his survival as he methodically planned his escape. He knew the three elements of fire—heat, fuel, and oxygen—were doing their deadly work as he sat, hopelessly trapped in the cage. Throughout his life Matt had been careful to maintain control of himself in every situation he encountered. Sitting in the fire, he knew—for the first time in his life—he wasn't in control.

His breathing took on a high-pitched sound as he tried to inhale the oxygen he stole from the fire. Feeling dizzy, he realized he was about to pass out. In one final act of desperation Matt pushed the safety bar off his lap. This shut off the engine as he attempted to climb out of the cage. As he lowered his head to exit, he realized he would have to crawl into the scorching, burning logs. He didn't like that option and sat back.

"I'm trapped!" he cried, panic racing through his veins. He thought of Melissa and the kids sleeping soundly in their beds.

"I'm in deep trouble," he thought as he reached back up and pulled the safety bar down over his lap. He turned the key and restarted the motor with the hope he could back out of the fire, which was already heating up his clothes. As the motor kicked into gear, the Bobcat smashed forward and deeper into the burning logs, sending hot embers high into the nighttime sky. The sudden shift also stoked the fire in the same way a person uses a poker.

When Matt turned on the ignition, the engine fan behind him sucked the horrendous flames and thick, deadly air toward him in pounding, all-enveloping waves. Now flames were overtaking the inside of the cage. He tried to figure out how he could use the Bobcat to free himself. In desperation he lifted the bucket that pulled the logs in closer to the machine and locked him in tighter.

Bang! A loud explosion rocked the tractor as the cylinders locked out. Now he couldn't raise or lower the bucket.

He looked down. Fire crept up his left leg. He searched

for a way out. He glanced around. His skin tingled from the heat. He had never felt so hopeless.

Matt choked back a sob. He'd never see his wife or kids again. Desperate as he sat in his fiery grave, he grabbed the cage with both hands, shook it as hard as he could, and screamed for help.

He didn't expect anyone to hear, much less respond. But Someone did.

From deep inside he heard the words, "You have twenty seconds to get out of this or it's over."

He screamed again, this time straining his vocal cords. He coughed, a puff of smoke escaping from his lungs.

Matt knew he sat at the front door of a hell of his own making. He was stuck—without the ability to do anything to save himself. But in this, his darkest hour, he could sense Jesus. No, he didn't see Him with his eyes. Instead he saw Him with his heart.

He took a final look at the flames. With determination he heard himself say, "You're going to have to crawl through that fire to get out."

As the flames painfully licked at his skin, he lifted the safety bar and turned his face to the right as far as he could. He crawled out and through the fire on his knees, left hand, and right forearm. He suffered first and second degree burns on the left side of his face. His legs and arms were burned too.

After remembering every minute detail from the time he left the house to the time he crawled into the fire, Matt remembers only snippets from the time he stepped into the fire to the time he woke up in the hospital many days later. One thing he doesn't remember is walking 198 steps—he counted later—uphill through the woods to his truck while everyone in his house slept peacefully. As Matt backed his truck out of the driveway, he reached for his cell phone and called his wife: "I'm so sorry. I've burned myself really bad. I'm seeing my hand melt away."

He called his parents: "I'm sorry. I've been hurt really bad. I'm headed to the emergency room."

He called 911: "I've been burned really bad. I'm on the way."

When Matt entered the emergency room door, a nurse met him. He barely remembered driving to the hospital. He looked around, stunned to find himself there.

"Chief, I need some help over here!" he heard a man say.

People started running, and Matt realized his situation must be worse than he thought.

They laid him on the stretcher and cut off his pants. A blister the size of a volleyball covered his left knee, and his left hand was literally dripping.

"I can't breathe." Matt struggled to spit out the words between gasps.

The emergency crew immediately inserted a tube into his charred mouth and down his throat before putting Matt into a drug-induced coma.

He spent the next several weeks unconscious in the burn unit where I worked an hour from his home. It was uncertain if he would survive the damage done to his lungs and body. His family prayed day and night. Though a slow and arduous process, Matt's recovery left the doctors and nurses ecstatic. None of us believed he would live through the horrible trauma his body had endured.

On the day he was scheduled to go home, nurses worked quickly to process his discharge in an effort to help celebrate his amazing recovery. The staff was accustomed to seeing death instead of recovery because burn patients in this particular unit were usually in the worst conditions and typically don't live. One final detail remained to complete. Matt would need home health care so nurses could evaluate and change the dressings on his wounds. As the paperwork was finalized, the doctor entered his room to discuss his plans for follow-up treatments.

"Are you left-handed?" a doctor asked Matt.

"No, sir."

"You know you had some help that night, don't you?"

"Yes, sir, the nurses and doctors…" Matt began.

"No. No. No. You had some greater help," the doctor interrupted. "Your right hand didn't have any debris and only minimal burns. It looks as if someone grasped your hand and pulled you out of the fire. Since you're right-handed, you would have used your dominant hand to reach out for help.

"Matt, you should have died," the doctor said, pointing up and smiling.

Matt began to put the pieces together. He knew he had no memory of getting out of the fire or walking through the woods to his truck. He didn't remember making any of the three calls during his drive to the emergency room. His wife and parents later told him of the conversations from that horrific night.

Weeks passed before he visited the emergency room staff to collect their memory of events. Listening to the 911 recording sent chills up his spine. His voice was calm and polite, almost as if someone else was talking. He had no memory of the conversation.

Matt knew Jesus had saved him from sure death. Matt hadn't been a faithful follower before the night of his accident. In fact, he lived five houses from the congregation he considered his home church but could recall going there only ten times in thirty-three years. And he wouldn't recognize the preacher—who had served there for twenty years—if he saw him on the street.

About three weeks after Matt had been admitted to the unit, I hurried by the nurse's station intending to catch up on my hourly documentation, when the secretary interrupted my thoughts. "Mr. Marion wants his nurse."

"OK, thanks," I said as I bypassed the free computer I'd intended to use. I walked into Matt's room with a big grin on my face. I enjoyed seeing his progress. It was refreshing to see someone actually recovering in the unit. The burn unit was a heart-wrenching place to work. The patients suffered indescribably, and the few that recovered were truly miracles.

"Hey, Matt, what'd you need?" I said as I thought of the mound of documentation that awaited me.

"Do you have a minute to sit down here and talk to me awhile?" He sounded a little discouraged.

I could sense he had something on his mind. I had cared for all types of patients in my many years of nursing, and not one had ever asked me to sit down and talk. My mind staggered at what could lie ahead.

"Sure," I said as I lowered myself onto the chair to his right. I was struggling with my remaining workload, but I knew I had to take time for Matt.

"I just wanted to talk to someone for a minute," he said.

"Sure. I enjoy talking with you. What's on your mind?" I crossed my hands in my lap in anticipation of what he might say. He told me the story of meeting his wife and how he loved being outdoors and playing sports. "You know, the scars that will be on my body don't bother me as much as the scars that will be on my legs. I love wearing my shorts."

All I could do was listen. I had no answers. Finally I

said, "Matt, you are blessed to be alive. God watched over you." Then I ventured a question. "Do you go to church?"

"Yeah, I go to church. I don't live like I should. I need to do better," he said.

"Are you saved, Matt?" I explored further.

"Yeah. I'm a Christian, but I need to do more for God."

We talked a few more minutes as I marveled at the wonder of the man before me. I had cared for Matt off and on for several weeks and was doubtful that he would ever go home. Today he sat in a recliner, a sweet smile on his face. His positive attitude always brightened our days.

Indeed, God is there when we need Him. Jesus says He will never leave or forsake us (Heb. 13:5). He says His sheep hear His voice and follow Him (John 10:27). In the darkest moments of his life, Matt's traumatic situation led him straight to his Savior. Deep in his heart on that dreadful night, he heard God's voice. He warned Matt he had only seconds to figure out a way to get free from his fiery grave, and He sent him an angel to pull him out. There is none like Him.

CHAPTER 19

AT-6 War Plane

I can do all things through Christ
which strengtheneth me.
—PHILIPPIANS 4:13, KJV

Y EARS AGO TODD's neighbor had rebuilt a World War II fighter plane, a two-seater with the cockpit in the front and the seat behind for the trainer pilot. The plane, an AT-6, was built with a canopy top in 1944.

The man, an accomplished commercial pilot with more than twenty-five years of experience, gave rides to neighbors and friends who attended an afternoon party to celebrate the completion of the plane. Todd was the fourth guest to fly. And the last.

Todd had never been an avid flier, but this was the opportunity of a lifetime to get to fly in a vintage WWII airplane. He had vertigo that day, so he was more concerned about not vomiting. The thought of crashing never crossed his mind.

He and the pilot took off and immediately flew across the Yadkin River before zipping back over the county where they both lived. They planned to buzz the hangar and then lift back into the air, much like pilots of the old-time aircrafts do at air shows.

On this run, however, the engine sputtered. The propellers stopped spinning. Todd could only hear the air whooshing past. At first he didn't realize what was happening. At one thousand feet all conversation stopped. The plane rolled and Todd grabbed the frame. His first thought was, "Here it goes. I'm going to be sick."

Right then the pilot leveled off the plane. Despite his modern headset, he didn't say a word. Time stood still. The next thing Todd remembers is seeing treetops and feeling erratic jolts.

The pilot headed for a nearby clearing but didn't make it. The plane started to roll, but the pilot was able to level it off again as they started into the trees. During the rapid descent Todd thought, "I'm going to unhook this seat belt so that when we go down I can get out quicker." Then he realized that unhooking the seat belt might launch him out of the plane and into a place he'd rather not be. As the plane hit the trees, the right wing clipped a limb and broke off. Fire roared through the cockpit. The plane smacked into the ground, belly-first but right side up.

After releasing his five-point buckle, Todd climbed out of the burning plane. A veteran firefighter, he knew he had only a moment to save the pilot, whose cockpit was now engulfed in flames. But the intensity of the fire forced Todd to give up his effort. Not able to save the pilot, Todd stumbled away from the plane, most of his upper body covered with burns. He soon would discover the worst damage was to his lungs.

Fortunately the plane had landed in a familiar setting, a wooded area he knew from his hunting days. He sat down and waited for rescue personnel to arrive. He knew the accident had happened close enough to the hanger that people would have seen the crash. Still, it took about fifteen minutes for help to arrive. The first person on the scene—another neighbor—found Todd sitting on a log with part of his parachute strap on.

Todd's adrenaline had kept the pain at bay, but he knew his burns were extensive. As chief of the local fire department, his greatest fear was being burned. He also worried about "his guys." Every time the department responded to a call, he prayed that none of them would get burned in the line of duty.

The first responders—many of them friends from the fire department and rescue teams—didn't recognize Todd at first. One of the firemen brought his pickup to the crash site, which was about a mile from the main road. Todd walked over to the truck and pulled himself onto the tailgate, where three guys joined him. He could hear the rescue chopper overheard but wasn't sure he wanted to fly again so soon. The lead paramedic on the scene—a friend of Todd's—didn't recognize him until he spoke. The medic jerked up his head and took a second look at Todd.

With an intubation kit in his hand, the medic asked if he should start the procedure on Todd, who said, "Go ahead. Do whatever you need to keep me alive."

The medic was unsure if starting a rapid sequence intubation was the right thing to do because he didn't know if Todd had inhalation burns. With any burn victim, possible burns in the throat and lungs are a concern. People who have inhaled smoke fumes often don't recover. The lungs are too delicate to handle fire.

To intubate Todd, the medics quickly sedated him. At the same time two other men started an IV in each foot because his arms were badly burned. Todd vaguely remembers the helicopter ride to the trauma center.

When he arrived at the emergency room, his arms were so swollen he was losing circulation in his extremities. The medical staff had to perform an emergency fasciotomy, a procedure in which the doctor makes a surgical incision to release pressure on the swelling extremity. They leave the incision open and apply sterile dressings to keep infection away. When the procedure was completed, Todd was transported to the tank room.

Todd doesn't have much recollection of the tank room either. He's probably better off not remembering. The tank room of a burn unit is where patients are showered and washed with soap to remove the trauma particles (dirt, grease, sand, etc.) from their burns and the scraping begins of third-degree eschar—charred dead skin.

Forty percent of Todd's body was covered with second- or

third-degree burns. He endured seventeen surgeries and spent a total of eighty-three days in the hospital.

Todd is alive today because of a miracle. A Christian since childhood, he admitted he had peace about the ordeal even as he walked—so to speak—through the fire. He craved food but couldn't eat because of the burns in his mouth. Yet he never entertained thoughts of death.

He has admitted many times since the accident that Philippians 4:13 kept him going and made him realize he could do this with God's help. Todd frequently said, "He'll get me through it."

I took care of Todd while he was in the burn unit. He endured horrible pain. His dressings had to be changed twice a day. He also endured physical therapy, baths, fittings for braces, occupational therapy, and more. Rarely have I seen someone so miserable. And every time he thought his pain might subside enough to sleep for a minute, someone else would come in to perform an ordered procedure. He never stopped hurting.

I wanted so badly to ask how he was feeling inside, but because of all his suffering, such a question seemed ridiculous. I felt terrible every time I changed his dressings. And with burns over 40 percent of his body, it took about forty-five minutes each time.

He wore his misery in every expression, every movement. I looked at his face and wanted to say, "Let's just not do this," but I knew that would ultimately cause more problems.

The support from his family and community was impressive. His wife was strong throughout the ordeal. Her faith never wavered, and she spent a great deal of time at the hospital to support and encourage Todd. His parents were at the hospital a lot too. Family and neighbors cared for

Todd's two sons by taking food to their home and the hospital. Todd's wall in the burn unit was covered with cards, pictures, posters, and signs of love from all his supporters. I don't believe I've ever seen a community come together the way this one did for Todd and his family.

Still, my heart ached for the suffering he endured. I wondered when he would ever leave the burn unit. My travel assignment ended before Todd's release, so I didn't know what happened to him and his family until years later.

Today Todd is doing well. Many of us agree his recovery is a true miracle.

✳ ✳ ✳

We often hear stories of miracles taking place overseas during revivals or mission trips. We often hear reports of people being raised from the dead, throwing off their crutches and walking for the first time in their lives, and other miraculous events.

My miracle came one cold, dark winter morning as I sped down the right lane of I-26 in North Carolina. I'm not a morning person, so leaving for work at five o'clock was always difficult for me. I got into my ice-cold car, placed my coffee cup in the holder, and set my cinnamon raisin bagel on the seat beside me. Within minutes I was cruising down the highway at sixty miles per hour. As I thought about the possibilities of the day ahead of me, I realized no other vehicles were on the interstate. I slowed my speed slightly and reached for the radio dial, thinking maybe there was something I should know.

As I returned my eyes to the road, I saw rows of bright red brake lights in my lane. I slowed a bit more, trying to adjust my eyes—and wishing I had put on my glasses so I could see better, I planned my strategy to pass if necessary. Within seconds I realized an eighteen-wheeler had stopped in my lane. I immediately pressed my brake and turned my wheel to pass, but my efforts were futile. The front wheels of my car began to skid.

I knew nothing of any bad weather. I hadn't watched or heard the weather, so the ice caught me by surprise. I took the appropriate maneuvers—letting off the gas and turning the car wheels in the opposite direction—to keep from wrecking. As I worked to get the car under control, I now understood the reason for the lack of traffic—bad weather. Then I realized I was headed directly toward the back end of a tractor-trailer. Thoughts of my family flashed through my mind. I gripped the steering wheel a little tighter.

"Well, this is it," I thought as I submitted to impending death. I closed my eyes tight and braced myself. There was nothing I could do but give in to whatever was going to happen. A few years earlier a younger cousin had instantly died when she slid into the front end of an eighteen-wheeler while traveling in a sudden snowstorm. She was only nineteen. I thought for a moment I was to meet the same fate.

After what seemed like an eternity, I thought I must be dead. I opened my eyes. To my amazement, I was still in my car, hands on the wheel, traveling down that steep mountain in the left-hand lane at fifty-five miles per hour.

And no truck in sight.

Trying to clear my thoughts, I wondered if I were dead and didn't have a grasp on it yet. Questions flooded my mind. "Is this what it's like to be dead? I'm stuck in time doing what I was doing before I died?"

Ten minutes later I pulled into the hospital's parking

deck and proceeded to my unit. On the way in I told myself, "OK, I have to be alive. Work is real."

I wanted to scream, "I'm alive!", while I jumped up and down. I still wasn't sure how it could be true. The only explanation was God's intervention.

A miracle.

God had transported me through natural space from the lane of sure death to the adjacent lane—the lane of the living.

My transport through space and time happened more than thirteen years ago, and every time I tell people about it, they stare in disbelief. The natural mind cannot comprehend the amazing things of God (Job 37:5).

At the moment we need Him, He is there. God promises to encamp His holy angels around us. He does this for our guidance and protection. He has given His angels the task of ministering to His people. These servants are here to help us when we cannot help ourselves.

I don't know what kind of angel protected me that morning, for by natural law the eighteen wheeler should have decapitated me. But God delivered me from sure death, and He'll do the same for you no matter what circumstances you face.

That morning the Lord spared me because my work for Him wasn't finished. Others who have experienced a miracle similar to mine, or have come back from the dead, all say the same thing. We read in Psalm 145:20, "The Lord preserves all those who love Him." Of course the Bible is full of miracles. The lists vary based on how the listmaker defines *miracle*. Regardless of the definition, God has a purpose for each one. In Bible times one reason for a miracle was to prove that the person performing it was sent by God. Another reason was to create faith in those who saw it.

I love the way Martin Luther King Jr. described faith when he said, "Faith is taking the first step even when you don't see the whole staircase."[1] When God leads us, we may not feel like it's the right thing, that we're not cut out for it. But when we follow Him up the staircase of our lives, one step at a time, He takes us where He wants us. As we begin our climb, we won't see the end results as our thighs burn, but if we stay obedient and faithful, we can keep going and one day see the purpose of all the hard work and suffering.

An entire book could be devoted to the miracles, some of which are better known than others: Jesus turning the water into wine, the healing of the woman with the issue of blood, Jesus feeding the five thousand, the casting out of demons. And let's not forget raising a widow's son from the dead at Nain or healing the leper.

Although the miracles experienced by Todd and me may never gain the fame of the numerous biblical miracles, they have had a tremendous impact on each of our lives. I'm sure it's safe to say our families are grateful we survived. And neither of us intends to stop talking about the great things God has done.

CHAPTER 20

Tunnel

And this is the message [the message of promise],
which we have heard from Him and now are
reporting to you: God is Light, and there
is no darkness in Him at all [no, not in any way].

—1 JOHN 1:5

EIGHT-YEAR-OLD SANDRA WAS excited to be going home to Winston-Salem from Mount Airy with her sister for the weekend. Her sister was twelve years older, and Sandra loved spending time with her. She loved the freedom of summer and the fun times they had together.

They decided to go to the community pool. Neither knew how to swim, but her sister loved lying by the pool while Sandra played in the shallow water.

"Sandra, don't you go into the deep water," her sister, Gaynell, said as she turned to lie on a lounge chair.

Gaynell settled into the chair and looked up. Sandra was gone.

Sandra had run on the ledge of the pool to the nine-foot-deep end. She climbed the metal steps, ran the length of the board, and jumped. She went down deep into the water. She scrambled to get back to the top. Her head barely broke the water line. She slipped back down into the water, splashing and hoping to get Gaynell's attention.

With no lifeguards on duty to save her, Sandra struggled to get back to the surface. She broke the surface again but only for a second. Her lungs aching, she scrambled back to the top again but quickly slipped back under—into a dark tunnel.

She was going down a dark tunnel. She continued along the path toward beams of intense bright light. A large group of children waited for her at the end of the tunnel. They smiled and held out their hands. Hoping they could help her, Sandra reached out and almost touched one of the children's hands when she felt the horrible pain of something pressing into her chest wall.

She looked up and saw people dressed in emergency uniforms standing over her. She heard her sister crying.

"She's gonna be OK," said a man in a uniform leaning over her.

Water poured from Sandra's throat and nose as she choked and coughed. The chlorine smelled and hurt. She wanted to throw up. She felt herself being lifted onto a stretcher. A bag was placed over her mouth and nose as she was rushed to the back of the ambulance. She could hear more people crying and orders for people to get out of the way being shouted. Sandra only wanted to close her eyes and never wake up.

Twenty-four hours later Sandra was released from the hospital, but the experience still haunts her and her sister to this day. Sandra will enter a swimming pool or ocean, but she'll only go in until the water reaches her waist. Her sister, Gaynell, however, has never been back to a swimming pool since.

✳ ✳ ✳

Aren't you thankful we have a redeeming God? Sometimes we all need a second chance—maybe three or four chances. This makes us grateful for our Lord's mercy and grace. No matter how difficult things are, we can find hope in Jesus. He promises that when we call, He will answer.

We all have endured our own personal hell at some point in life. For some that may have been the loss of a loved one. For others it might have been a bad marriage. The suffering we experience in these darkest moments of our lives pale in comparison to spending eternity without God.

We should remember our affliction lasts only but a moment in the vast scope of time. When the circumstances of life have us down, we just need to call upon His name.

And it shall be that whoever shall call upon the name of the Lord [invoking, adoring, and worshipping the Lord—Christ] shall be saved.

—Acts 2:21

God is always there for us. Call on Him.
It's never too late.

CHAPTER 21

Field of Flowers

For it was in Him that all things were created, in
heaven and on earth, things seen and things unseen,
whether thrones, dominions, rulers, or authorities; all
things were created and exist through Him [by His
service, intervention] and in and for Him.

—COLOSSIANS 1:16

EVENTY-EIGHT-YEAR-OLD PAUL CHECKED into the hospital January 1996 for what should have been a routine colonoscopy the next day. Doctors wanted to have a day to monitor his health as Paul had an enlarged heart, and congestive heart failure was prevalent in the family.

Paul's wife, Anna, accompanied him and spent the day with him as the nurses and doctors got him settled into his room and prepped for the next day. As the afternoon gave way to the evening, Anna needed to head home. She suffered from macular degeneration, a disease that makes it difficult to see at night.

"Honey, I'm going to go home," she said. "It's getting dark."

Tired but in good spirits Paul said, "OK, you go on home."

Anna gathered her things and kissed him good night, the same type of kiss she had given him thousands of times during their fifty-four years of marriage. She paused at the door, turned, gave him a smile, and walked out.

Within minutes Paul and his roommate were chatting away like lifelong chums. But in midsentence Paul suddenly stopped.

Paul and Anna later learned that the roommate looked over to see Paul hanging his head, chin resting on his chest. The alarm sounded on Paul's heart monitor. The roommate pushed the call button for the nurses.

Two scrambled into the room, not sure of the problem. The heart monitor Paul was hooked up to sometimes would sound an alarm because of artifact from rapid movement, such as brushing one's teeth or hair. Or the alarm can sound when something has happened to the patient's heart rhythm or rate.

The nurses discovered Paul was in full respiratory arrest and his heart had stopped.

"No pulse. No breathing. Start CPR!" a nurse yelled as she pressed the code button on the wall.

A handful of other health care team members ran in. Paul's doctor arrived a few minutes later. Working strategically and feverishly, they took mere minutes to revive Paul. In situations like this any delay in getting oxygen to the brain and other vital organs can cause permanent damage. When they stabilized his vital signs, Paul was put on a respirator and moved to the intensive care unit.

About twenty minutes after she left the hospital, Anna received a call detailing the news of Paul's decline in health. Despite her fear of driving at night, she rushed back to the hospital.

Meanwhile Paul's daughter, Sharyn, a nurse who lived in another state, had called numerous times throughout the day. She wanted a moment to talk with him and to allow her children time as well. Finally she reached someone who connected her with her mother in the ICU waiting room. Anna recounted the details to Sharyn about what had happened.

"Sharyn, Paul is not responding," Anna said, fear and concern obvious in her voice.

Nervously Sharyn said, "I'll come up."

"No, no, no," Anna said. "Don't come up. They said we'll know in twenty-four hours."

"Let me tell you one thing," Sharyn said, gaining strength. "Whatever you do, talk to him. Tell him that you love him and just talk to him."

Sharyn often suggested to her own patients' families to talk to loved ones who had been revived.

"OK," Anna said before she hung up.

Two days later Paul recovered and was transferred to a step-down unit. One week later he was discharged home without having his colonoscopy.

In August of that year the family gathered at Paul's house to celebrate his birthday. Paul and Sharyn made their way out to the porch for father-daughter alone time.

"I don't understand what happened to me that day," Paul said with a look of concern on his face.

"Well, what do you remember?" Sharyn asked.

A man of few words, Paul answered in a slow and measured tone. "Well, all I remember was your mother and I were out on a ride, and we stopped by the side of the road because the sunlight was so beautiful and a field of big yellow daisies just made us want to walk in them. I got out of the car to walk in that field of flowers. The sunlight was so warm and comforting I just wanted to go there. It was drawing me there.

"But, dang it, your mother kept calling me back."

CHAPTER 22

The Cage

And there is salvation in and through no one else, for
there is no other name under heaven given among
men by and in which we must be saved.

—ACTS 4:12

FOR WEEKS I had dreaded this day. I paused outside the room of a burn victim in intensive care burn unit who tried to kill herself eight months before by driving head-on into a tractor-trailer. As the new nurse on the floor, I knew at some point the night shift charge nurse would assign me to care for Cassi.

Third-degree burns covered 90 percent of her body. Most people who have injuries this severe don't survive. Cassi endured multiple surgeries in an attempt to graft some skin to her raw muscles. Deadly infections postponed scheduled surgeries numerous times. Now an invalid, she depended on others for her every need. Each time anyone attempted to turn her or clean her wounds, she cried out in pain. Yet Cassi hung on for a reason we couldn't comprehend.

And I would be the one to find out why.

I learned from the other nurses that at the time of her wreck, Cassi was a twenty-eight-year-old wife and mother of three. She teetered on the edge of despair after losing her job as a secretary and hearing her husband confess to an affair and then ask for a divorce. Alcohol and anti-depressants became her best friends. She lost the mental and physical energy to care for her children. When she finally decided her life wasn't worth living, she walked to the bathroom sink, took a handful of antidepressants, and washed them down with a long drink of vodka. Tears streaming down her face, she grabbed the keys to her Honda Civic and walked out the door.

A short time later she raced down a nearby two-lane road. Impatient with the driver in front of her, Cassi swung into the opposite lane to pass. Through tear-filled eyes, she saw an eighteen-wheeler bearing down on her. "It's now or never," she thought as she mentally replayed the last argument she had with her husband. She sobbed, pulled in a quick breath, and—fury raging deep in her soul—accelerated.

* * *

Cassi tried to focus. When the fog in her mind cleared, she realized she was in a cage.

And not alone.

An indeterminable number of hideous creatures swarmed around her, tormenting, pointing, and laughing at her.

Feelings of being lost, bewildered, and alone swirled in her mind like ingredients in a blender.

* * *

The team of nurses caring for her felt Cassi would've been better off had she not survived the crash. But she did. At the scene paramedics revived her despite her horrific condition. And now she lay badly burned in the room behind the glass door in front of me, two states away from her home, family, and friends, with a secret that tormented her daily. I gathered my courage, said a little prayer, and walked through the door.

"Hey, Cassi," I said, still trying to gather more courage to face her. "My name is Liz. I'll be taking care of you today."

She looked at me with a level of pain that broke my heart. In all my years of nursing I've never seen so much fear and terror in one person's eyes.

Patients in her condition value and need the stability of being cared for by the same people day in and day out. Changing personnel often causes a brief time of anxiety or panic. I sensed her apprehension that day and feared a new nurse might be too much for her to handle.

I was having trouble myself. The sight of her was almost too much for me to handle. I wanted to run. Her body stiff from the neck down, she could move only her upper extremities, neck, mouth, and eyes. Her upper extremities looked more skeletal than human. Paper-thin, scarred skin stretched to cover her arms, hands, and fingers, like lacey material across the bones grafted together from multiple operations.

I couldn't imagine having the will to live in such a horrible condition. It struck me as odd she didn't have a DNR (Do Not Resuscitate order), particularly since she had tried to take her own life.

Now I regretted taking the travel assignment. What was I thinking? I had never wanted to work in the burn unit, yet here I was, standing near a patient in worse shape than anyone I'd ever seen. I wanted to cancel this assignment and deal with the loss, but I couldn't because of the hardship it would cause my family. I felt like a sacrificial lamb.

Trying to mask my own pain of seeing Cassi for the first time, I systematically assessed her intravenous fluids and the central line—used for her IV medications—in the right side of her chest. As I continued my assessment, she flapped her arms in a dramatic fashion. When she caught my full attention, she mouthed three words that I couldn't quite make out because of the tracheotomy in her throat.

"What?" I asked, my pulse quickening. I was not only dealing with the assignment to care for a person in this shape but also with the frustration of not being able to communicate with her. With the fear and anxiety in her eyes escalating, she mouthed the three words again.

Frustrated, I said, "I can't understand, Cassi." She

pointed to a pad and pencil. I retrieved both and placed them in her left hand as she lay with her head elevated about thirty degrees.

With all her strength Cassi took the pad and pencil and scribbled, "I can't breathe." As soon as she finished writing, she stopped breathing.

I was terrified. My mind locked up. I stared at her for a moment as I tried to get the gears in my head to start working again. Then it clicked. I knew what to do. I called out, my voice barely above a whisper, "I need help in here!"

This was rapidly becoming more than I could handle. For one thing, I'd never been responsible for anyone in such a horrible condition. I also feared the usual staff in the unit might think I was unreliable because I hadn't noticed what Cassi was trying to tell me.

Then I pushed the call bell. When no one answered, it dawned on me the rest of the staff might've been burnt out from caring for Cassi. As I mentioned before, she was a difficult case, and I found out later that Cassi pushed the button for assistance a lot each day. If I had been thinking clearly, I would've pushed the Code button. That's the button we push for immediate help. Desperate, I walked to the unit doorway and gasped again, "I need help in here!"

At last the charge nurse, not realizing the gravity of the situation, wandered into Cassi's room. She immediately grabbed the breathing bag (Ambu bag) from the hanger on the wall and began resuscitating Cassi and called for more help. An Ambu bag provides ventilation to a patient who is not breathing or is struggling to breathe. The device is an essential part of our crash cart.

It took four of us—the charge nurse, a nursing assistant, respiratory therapist, and me—to save Cassi. We also put her back on the breathing machine, considered somewhat of a setback after the staff had attempted to wean her off it.

But I had a greater concern and burden: the condition of her soul. Nine years earlier I wasted the opportunity to share the gospel with a patient (Mr. Smith, see chapter 1). I never wanted to make that mistake again. What if she died and I didn't know if she knew Jesus? I couldn't bear the thought!

It took us about fifteen minutes to get Cassi stabilized. Within a few more minutes she could communicate with me again. When I was sure she could think clearly, I asked if she believed in Jesus Christ. She told me no and that she didn't know much about religion, although she'd grown up in a Catholic school. She said she had never read any of the Bible and knew very little about Jesus Christ.

I told her Jesus died on the cross for her sins and rose again on the third day so she could be free and go to heaven when her time came to die. I asked if she wanted to know Him. A happy river of tears streamed down her scarred face as she nodded. Then, along with me, she mouthed a prayer of salvation. As she completed the prayer, Cassi indicated she wanted to tell me something but was afraid I might question her sanity.

To this day I'm not sure why she chose me. Though she never spoke again after the wreck, she was able to share her story by writing answers to my questions. I didn't have much time—probably less than five minutes—because I had to care for another patient.

When I assured Cassi I wouldn't doubt her sanity or the validity of the story, she began writing it out. Now I understood why she refused to die. She lived in constant fear of going back to the cage should she die again.

She fought every day to stay alive in the hope of finding a remedy, peace, or deliverance.

Because of her injuries Cassi couldn't explain the details of her ordeal. It didn't matter. The Bible describes hell in ways that helped me imagine her fear: "And the smoke of their torment ascends forever and ever; and they have no respite (no pause, no intermission, no rest, no peace) day or night..." (Rev. 14:11)

No wonder Cassi was so determined to stay alive despite the severity of her wounds.

In his book *23 Minutes in Hell* Bill Wiese describes the horrific torture of eternal damnation. At 3:00 a.m. on November 23, 1998, he was hurled into the air and landed in what appeared to be a prison cell. Like others who have had similar experiences, he describes the experience in gruesome detail. I say gruesome because he was in hell. The torture he suffered far exceeded anything he ever experienced on the earth. Since he returned from that experience, he has made it his mission to educate people on the horrendous life of eternity without Christ.

After sharing her experience in the cage, Cassi's countenance changed. When I cared for her, she always asked me to read from the Bible. Her favorite verse was Isaiah 40:31 (KJV): "But they that wait upon the LORD shall renew their strength; they shall mount up with wings as eagles; they shall run, and not be weary; and they shall walk, and not faint." Although her physical body was still miserable, her spirit had changed.

As shown in the Acts 4 passage, Peter proclaimed to the high priests and elders that the power and authority of Jesus Christ is the only way to salvation. There is no other.

Cassi had a firsthand experience of this truth the day she decided to drive into the eighteen-wheeler. Because she didn't understand the salvation Jesus had for her and had not known Him, her soul experienced unfathomable torture when she died. For the soul without Jesus, worse things than death await.

Remember the story about the rich man and Lazarus from Luke 16:19–31? The rich man enjoyed his life here on earth, and the beggar Lazarus suffered inconsolably. The rich man died and left us with an eyewitness account of the torment one experiences in hell. Tortured by the flames, the rich man lifted up his eyes one day and saw Abraham far away with Lazarus at his bosom. The rich man cried out for pity and mercy, but none came. He asked Abraham to let Lazarus dip the tip of his finger in water to cool his tongue, but Abraham said, "Between us and you a great chasm has been fixed, in order that those who want to pass from this [place] to you may not be able" (v. 26).

Despite persistent begging, even for a warning for his five brothers, the rich man didn't get his wish. He missed out. God gives us plenty of chances, and apparently the rich man passed them all up.

Cassi, on the other hand, made the most of her chance. She survived a massive explosion—solely by the grace of God. After her life-after-death experience, she refused to die again. Terrified of the realm of the dead, she was determined to live in her mangled body. She never felt the painful impact of the crash, never felt the intense flames of the explosion, and never smelled the blood being spilled or the stench of flesh being burned.

What she did feel was the pain of confinement. She immediately found herself imprisoned in an old cage, tortured by hideous creatures. These were demons assigned to torture her for eternity.

Cassi suffered physically and spiritually through many

long months. We changed her bandages twice a day. She couldn't lie in the same position for long periods of time. Sleep didn't come easily. But the worst suffering by far was the torment of slipping into an eternal hell. Still, Cassi got a second chance. She finally found the peace for which she longed.

Two weeks later Cassi gave up the fight. She chose eternity with Jesus instead of a life of constant suffering. She let go.

It's never too late for us to give our life to the Lord. As He did with Cassi, Jesus can heal us. Many people are afraid to confess their sins because they feel they've committed far more than the Lord is willing to forgive. But the truth is He forgives it all.

We shouldn't allow fear to keep us from seeking salvation. Death will be worse than living if we do not know Jesus as our Savior. No matter how difficult things are, we can find hope in Jesus. Though our flesh—the outer man—may die, our spirits live on forever in eternity if we are committed to following the ways and teachings of Jesus Christ.

CHAPTER 23

Warning

I will bless the Lord, Who has given me counsel: yes,
my heart instructs me in the night seasons.

—PSALM 16:7

O NE NIGHT A few years ago I had a dream about a flood that washed out a road my family and I traveled daily. In the dream my husband and oldest daughter were swept away. Naturally this dream troubled me all day

Like Nebuchadnezzar I couldn't get my dream off my mind. The next morning I went off to work my usual twelve-hour shift. That day nothing much happened— just the ordinary stuff that a nurse deals with: taking vital signs, passing out meds, doing reports, and cleaning up a mess or two. Most importantly I spent time taking care of my patients and their needs.

Near the end of the day I received an unusual call from my husband. He wanted to take me out to dinner after work. I worked an hour away in Asheville, North Carolina. I didn't want him to make that drive, particularly with our two young daughters. Plus money had been tight for some time, so I thought it odd that he wanted to treat me. Tim was attending Fruitland Baptist Bible Institute in Hendersonville, North Carolina, at the time and making very little money working part-time at a local Nautilus gym.

I didn't want to spend money going out to dinner. And I didn't want to leave my car in the hospital parking deck for the weekend. But after a little convincing, I agreed to let Tim take me to dinner.

He arrived with our disgruntled daughters, Tabitha and Jessi, who were at each other's throats from the long boring ride, about an hour later. We set out for seafood at Joe's. The drive was just thirty minutes or so, but we were slowed by a driving rain that made it difficult for Tim to see the highway and the exit signs.

When we arrived at the restaurant, we dashed from the

car to the front door but still got drenched. While we ate, I was nervous about the rain. I hoped it would let up while we ate trout, chicken strips, and shrimp. To our dismay the rain did not lighten up, but we decided to continue on our way home anyway. As we approached our exit ramp thirty minutes later, the dream I had the night before came back to me. I suggested to Tim, "Maybe we should take the other road home."

Without hesitating, he agreed. He sped past that exit and took the next one. Although the extra distance added another ten minutes to our drive, it was worth it. I was able to relax for the first time since having the dream the night before.

The next morning I found out from friends that the road on our normal route (the one we would have used when returning from the restaurant) had flooded over. A moment of panic washed over me, followed by a crashing wave of relief that God had used the dream to warn me to not use our normal road.

* * *

Sometimes we need to pause and consider the amazing things of God. We didn't share this experience with a lot of people, at first. We just pondered it in our hearts. Sometimes His divine intervention is too much for us to comprehend, and sometimes we fear people will not believe us anyway. I encourage you to tell others about the amazing things God does for you—or to at least recognize the things He does.

A friend of mine and his wife started a praise calendar a number of years ago when things weren't going well. It helped remind them of the amazing things God does do.

After a year or so they looked back through the preceding months and relived some of the events. Some were big; others, small. It didn't matter. When God did something in their lives, they wrote it down.

After a while they started looking and keeping their eyes open to what God was doing in their lives. They sat and talked about it. One of the bigger blessings came from a friend who paid the airfare for one of them to visit their son in another state. Others were small, like a mixed-up order at a restaurant that yielded a free appetizer.

No matter what, God says to give Him the glory. The more we do this, the more amazing things will happen in our lives. Give the credit where it belongs—all to Jesus. You may help someone else become curious enough about His goodness that they'll draw near to Him too.

So don't be shy. Talk. Write. Share your experiences. That's why God gives us experiences—so we can help and encourage others, particularly if they are going through a difficult situation similar to what we've experienced at some point in our lives.

CHAPTER 24

LeRoy

You believe that God is one; you do well. So do the
demons believe and shudder [in terror and horror
such as make a man's hair stand on end and
contract the surface of his skin]!

—JAMES 2:19

DURING A THREE-WEEK span in 2010 Josh woke up almost every night at 1:05 a.m. in a cold sweat—nauseated, confused, and angry. Each time the dream started the same way—with Josh on his usual shift, patrolling the I-74 connector with US 52 in North Carolina that runs east-west near Mount Airy. While sitting at mile marker six, he clocked a speeding car traveling well over the limit. He turned on his siren, pulled out, and took off after the lawbreaker. After a short chase the car pulled to the side of the interstate. Josh called in the license plate to the dispatcher, collected his paperwork, and walked to the driver's side window to ask for a license and vehicle registration card.

The driver reached into the glove box to retrieve the requested documents. When he turned back around, he aimed a small pistol at Josh's chest and pulled the trigger. Heat immediately flashed through Josh's body as he fell to the ground. Blood poured from the open wound, staining his blue uniform shirt. He knew he was going to die alongside this major interstate in broad daylight. The murdering motorist sped away as Josh struggled to maintain consciousness. He could feel his soul drifting from his body.

He was overcome by the knowledge he would never see his family again. Never have a wife or children. Never see another sunrise. The worst part, though, was feeling his soul sliding into hell.

There he was assigned to cell number nine on level 616. Each cell, like those in jails and prisons on the earth, had three walls with the only entrance through the bars at the front. Unlike the atmosphere in a normal jail cell, it was pitch dark, hot, and muggy, making it difficult to breathe. Yet he was aware of everything around him despite not being able to see.

That was the good part.

The bad part? Each cell contained the occupant's worst fears. The prisoner to his right was in a pit of snakes; the one to his left was constantly falling. Josh's cell was full of spiders. All his life he was terrified of the eight-legged creatures, big or small. In hell he was tormented day and night by the spiders that covered every inch of the walls and floor.

To keep the prisoners in check, a demon stood guard outside each cell. LeRoy was stationed outside of Josh's cell. Although he couldn't see him while in his cell, Josh sensed the demon's presence. That tortured him almost as much as the spiders. Josh felt so helpless and alone. His life was drained from him, no hope. He knew it would be that way forever.

While in hell Josh never thought of his family, friends, or God. All his energy and focus were directed to the torment caused by the spiders and the presence of LeRoy.

Each day at noon the devil, Satan himself, visited Josh in his cell. LeRoy would unlock the bars, and then Satan would escort Josh supernaturally from level 616 to level 646 to an identical cell. Between 6:00 p.m. and 9:00 p.m. each evening Josh was transported back to level 616.

Josh described the devil as a clean-cut, good-looking manlike creature with short brown hair, a deep chilling voice, a goatee, and, not surprisingly, tanned skin. He stood about five-feet-eleven with an average build.

During his visits the devil kept his eyes glued on Josh, even when he talked with LeRoy. Try as he might, hideous screams of the captives in adjacent cells kept Josh from being able to hear any of the conversations between the two sinister beings. So each afternoon Josh remained confined to the cell on level 646 watching the devil and LeRoy converse.

Each night, after Josh had been returned to his cell on level 616, the dream ended with the devil lunging at Josh. He awoke with a start, usually in a pool of sweat.

The dream motivated Josh to search for its meaning. His search led him to church.

✳ ✳ ✳

Accounts of hell are terrifying. People who dream of eternal damnation or supernaturally visit this place of torment often end up changed. Many believe these visions of hell are one way our heavenly Father guides us to a Christian life. By showing people their eternal fate, He gives them a warning that they need to change their ways because He doesn't want anyone to perish.

John 10:28 says, "And I give them eternal life, and they shall never lose it or perish throughout the ages. [To all eternity they shall never by any means be destroyed.] And no one is able to snatch them out of My hand."

He wants to show His mighty love and affection for us. He desires to communicate with us and surprise us with His amazing power. Through His supernatural ways and means of communication we can have a relationship with God that is immeasurable. He desires to spend time with us, speak to us, and shower His mercy on us every day of our lives. He not only communicates with us, but He also communicates *big* when we need it.

CHAPTER 25

His Splendor

And we [have seen and] know [positively] that the
Son of God has [actually] come to this world and has
given us understanding and insight [progressively] to
perceive (recognize) and come to know better and
more clearly Him Who is true; and we are in Him
Who is true—in His Son Jesus Christ (the Messiah).
This [Man] is the true God and Life eternal.

—1 JOHN 5:20

FㅤOR MONTHS JESSI craved a deeper relationship with the Holy Spirit. On October 31, 2010, while the congregation sang "You are Welcome in this Place" by Hillsong, the pastor told the people in attendance to raise their hands. My daughter did, along with the rest of the congregation. Later Jessi told us she was "already being overwhelmed by the Holy Spirit."

Not only was Jessi singing the words, she was also crying out for the Holy Spirit to come be with her. The Holy Spirit knows the difference between just singing a song and meaning what you're singing. Since summer Jessi had longed for a deeper relationship with the Holy Spirit. This desire started when she went with my husband, Tim, and me to a camp meeting. A popular evangelist spoke the last night. Jessi was particularly impressed with how this evangelist spoke as though he personally knew the Holy Spirit, and he knew things she couldn't imagine knowing. She told the Lord that night, "I want to know You the way he knows You."

Now a few months later, on the last Sunday in October, she cried out again for an experience with the Holy Spirit. She was open and willing. He did not let her down.

Midway through the song she rose from her seat and walked to the front of the church. Our pastor began to pray over her and said, "The Holy Spirit is getting ready to take you on a journey." The words were barely out of his mouth when Jessi crumbled to the floor. She said the presence of the Holy Spirit was so rich and precious she just wanted to lie there, basking in His presence and the love He lavished over her. While she remained sprawled out on the floor with others praying around her, the Holy Spirit told her softly, "Follow Me."

When she replied in her next breath, "As long as You

are there with me, I'll go," the Holy Spirit took her on a journey to the throne, an uncomfortable place where she couldn't see Him, a beautiful meadow, then underneath a shady tree. During her time with the Holy Spirit she experienced a roller-coaster ride of emotions: joy, grieving, love, pain, bliss, sorrow, and a sense of urgency.

She visited the throne room of God as a four-year-old child, her long blonde hair hanging to the middle of her back. With the indefinable form of the Holy Spirit holding her hand, she approached two men sitting on thrones. She knew they were the Father and His Son, Jesus. She walked toward the Father. He picked her up and sat her on His lap, where she leaned on His chest and hugged Him. She was overwhelmed by His love and never wanted to leave. But being curious like a child of that age, she went to Jesus. She crawled up into His lap for a moment and then hopped down to hold His hand and play around His legs.

The Holy Spirit then took Jessi to a place dominated by cloudy shades of gray, black, and red. The mood shifted from one of playfulness to a serious tone. Here she learned of the urgency to "tell them." When the Holy Spirit repeated the command, Jessi saw people and villages around the world she'd never even seen before. The Holy Spirit then said, "Tell them about Jesus and that He died for them so that they might be free from their sins and live in heaven with Him someday and have life everlasting."

The Holy Spirit continued to instruct her, "If you had a child, you wouldn't want her to die. I feel the same way when My children die and go to hell. I don't want My children to die. Tell them Jesus died for them."

She wept loudly, her body rocked by gentle convulsions as she curled into a fetal position.

Still on the floor, Jessi could faintly hear someone praying over her. The person prayed in earnest at first but became selfish before Jessi realized the distraction had caused her to miss precious time with the Holy Spirit. When she turned her focus back on the Holy Spirit, begging Him not to leave because of the commotion, He angrily replied, "People come to church every Sunday, then during the week they are all about themselves. They then come back the next Sunday the same way they were the week before. It's a cycle. People get a touch from my Holy Spirit, then go and do what they want. They are grieving Me."

She wept again.

"Every Sunday the people in the church come with their petty problems while people are dying and going to hell," the Holy Spirit continued, with such compassion and concern she had never seen or heard before. "Tell them, Jessi."

The setting changed again—this time to a meadow where she and the Holy Spirit walked to the middle. He picked a blade of grass and, with a somber expression, said, "Life is like a blade of grass. People think they have all the time in the world when they really don't. You have to tell them, Jessi."

Then the Holy Spirit asked about the kitten she received two days prior. Our oldest daughter, Tabitha, had married her love, Eddie, earlier that year and took the family cat along with her to her new home. Jessi begged my husband and me for another cat. While we debated whether or not we wanted one, Jessi's boyfriend surprised her with a kitten. A huge animal lover, she fell in love with the soft bundle of fur right away.

Now, as she stood in the middle of the meadow, the Holy Spirit asked, "Your new kitten is cute, isn't he?" After she responded, the Holy Spirit said, "I want people to be like your kitten. He follows you wherever you go. I want people to follow Me the way the kitten follows its keeper."

Jessi's Holy Spirit experience concluded under a shady tree where she asked questions about Jesus and heaven. Each time the Holy Spirit answered in a loving and kind voice, much like a best friend forever might. As He walked Jessi back to the church, she heard an exuberant woman sharing her experience with the Holy Spirit. He confided, "I like to make people happy and laugh."

Experiences like this often inspire people to seek more of our heavenly Father. We must understand God the Father sends the Holy Spirit to help us through our lives. As part of the holy Trinity, the Holy Spirit is more than just a spirit or thing we can call up through a séance or Ouija board. He is a real person of the Godhead, and we are indwelt by the Holy Spirit. That means the Holy Spirit lives in us.

We have a number of scriptures to show the coexistence of the entities within the Trinity. In Luke 3:22 we read, "And the Holy Spirit descended upon Him in bodily form like a dove, and a voice came from heaven, saying, You are My Son, My Beloved! In You I am well pleased and find delight!"

Also, in Mark 1:10-13 we read, "And when He came up out of the water, at once he [John] saw the heavens torn open and the [Holy] Spirit like a dove coming down [to enter] into Him. And there came a voice out from within heaven, You are My Beloved Son; in You I am well pleased. Immediately the [Holy] Spirit [from within] drove Him out into the wilderness (desert), and He stayed in the wilderness (desert) forty days, being tempted [all the while] by Satan; and He was with the wild beasts, and the angels ministered to Him [continually]."

This helps us to understand the Holy Spirit is a person, not an "it" or "a force." The Holy Spirit, who proceeds from the Father, is capable of leading us into all truth. For this to happen, we need to be open and willing to receive His guidance and direction. We just need spiritual ears to hear and spiritual eyes to see.

When we begin to see things through our spiritual eyes, we have things revealed to us by the Holy Spirit. Whether through death, sickness, or the amazing mysteries of dreams and visions, God shows Himself in our lives as we recognize His greatness during our yearning to hear from Him.

Many websites and other books are available to help interpret a vision or dream. That's not my goal here. The experiences within this book are shared to help draw you into a deeper relationship with God, whether you're new to faith or have been following Jesus since childhood. I also hope these stories will encourage a nonbeliever to make a decision for Christ. Whatever the case may be, supernatural encounters and experiences are designed for a purpose that will undoubtedly change not only your life but also the lives of the people around you.

Imagine for a moment the joy of the experience, if you haven't already, from a visit from an angel or seeing a vision of Jesus. It could happen at any time. At any place. God's love knows no boundaries. Nor does He wait until we're ready. Remember, His ways are not our ways. And His timing often differs dramatically from ours.

The first step is to cry out to God. He hears the heart that cries out to Him. Some cry out, "If You are real, show me," and He does. Whenever we cry out with a humble, repentant heart, He hears. If you've never asked Jesus Christ to come into your heart but you know there is more to life than what you have, now is the time. I urge you to pray this simple prayer and become His child. He will come to live in you and fill your life with amazing wonders you never imagined possible. He has everything you need. He means to give all His goodness to you.

Pray this with your heart:

Lord Jesus, I know I haven't always done things right. I admit I am a sinner, and I am asking You to forgive me of my sins. I regret that I ever hurt You, and I regret that I have lived my life carelessly. I ask You to come into my heart and my life and be Lord of my life. Take me and mold me into someone You can use to bless others. I open my heart and life to Your wonderful ways. Thank You, Lord Jesus, for saving me. You are my God, and I serve only You. In Jesus's name, amen.

If you prayed this prayer and want to experience more of God and His great wonders, I urge you get a Bible and start reading it. Proverbs is a great place to start, and the Holy Spirit will lead you from there. I like the Amplified version of the Bible because it expands the meanings of Greek and Hebrew words. It helps me understand the message more clearly and apply it to my life. But many versions are available, so choose the one that best fits your own reading style.

Next begin praying for God to lead you to a church home that will teach you more about the awesome God we serve. Finding the right church is essential. There you will meet other new Christians as well as seasoned believers who can help you grow in Christ. I do want to caution that a good church can be difficult to find. Make sure you visit churches that teach the truths of Jesus Christ as you search out the one that will be your home.

Don't delay or avoid this important step. As you read, pray, and consistently learn from other Christians, you will find the joy and excitement of following God. As He pours out His Spirit upon you, you'll experience His supernatural interventions and wonders in your life too.

It's important to understand what to do once we have invited Jesus into our lives and hearts. His love is the greatest love we will ever experience. He sends His Holy Spirit to remain within us and as our confidant, comforter, guide, and best friend at all times to prove His great love. The Holy Spirit works within us as we read the Bible, go to church, and ask Him what He wants for our lives. He will show us our purpose. And He will guide us into that purpose as we are willing and obedient to God the Father's instructions.

Jesus never did anything without the Father showing Him what to do, and we are to follow His example (John 12:49–50). In the introduction I mentioned I came across this scripture one night when needing to make an important decision about my career. I realized that night that this scripture was a powerful component to my purpose in life. Because of that I wrote this book.

NOTES

INTRODUCTION

1. United States Department of Labor Bureau of Statistics, "Table 6. The 30 Occupations With the Largest Projected Employment Growth, 2010-20," http://www.bls.gov/news.release/ecopro.t06.htm (accessed March 9, 2012).

2. Nancy Gibbs and Richard N. Ostling, "God's Billy Pulpit," *Time*, November 15, 1993, http://www.time.com/time/magazine/article/0,9171,979573,00.html (accessed March 9, 2012).

3. Barry M. Horstman. "Man With a Mission," *Cincinnati Post*, June 27, 2002.

4. Thinkexist.com, "Thomas Alva Edison Quotes," http://thinkexist.com/quotation/opportunity_is_missed _by_most_people_because_it/12130.html (accessed March 9, 2012).

CHAPTER 19 · AT-6 WAR PLANE

1. Thinkexist.com, "Martin Luther King Jr. Quotes, http://thinkexist.com/quotation/faith_is_taking_the _first_step_even_when_you_don/214973.html (accessed March 12, 2012).